ONLY BY DIVINE DESIGN

*Two downed planes, two parachutes,
one school shooting,
and a mustard seed of faith*

DORENE STARK

FOREWORD BY MICHAEL LEWIS, AUTHOR, *THE BLIND SIDE*

STELLAR STUDIO
LITTLETON, CO

———∽———

*This book is dedicated to my family,
for present and future generations to come.*

*It is also dedicated to those
who long to see God in their life.*

————————————

THE MIRACLES THAT HAPPEN IN THE DAILY LIVES OF THOSE WHOM GOD HAS CALLED ARE HAPPENING IN EVERY MOMENT OF EVERY DAY, EVERYWHERE.

CONTENTS

Forward by Michael Lewis ix

Preface xiii

Acknowledgments xxi

Introduction xxiii

1. Bailout! 1
2. Change of Course 13
3. Blanket of Protection 25
4. Miracle Births 33
5. The Spin 57
6. The Massacre 71
7. The Hunt 105
8. Captured 117
9. The Shepherd 135
10. Heading to Lakenheath 161
11. Timely Meetings 183
12. Welcome Home 189
13. God Moves the Mountain 207
14. In the Stillness 219

Afterword 227

Divine Moments in Time 253

    Reconciliation 255

    My Horse, My Teacher 261

    Car Accident 273

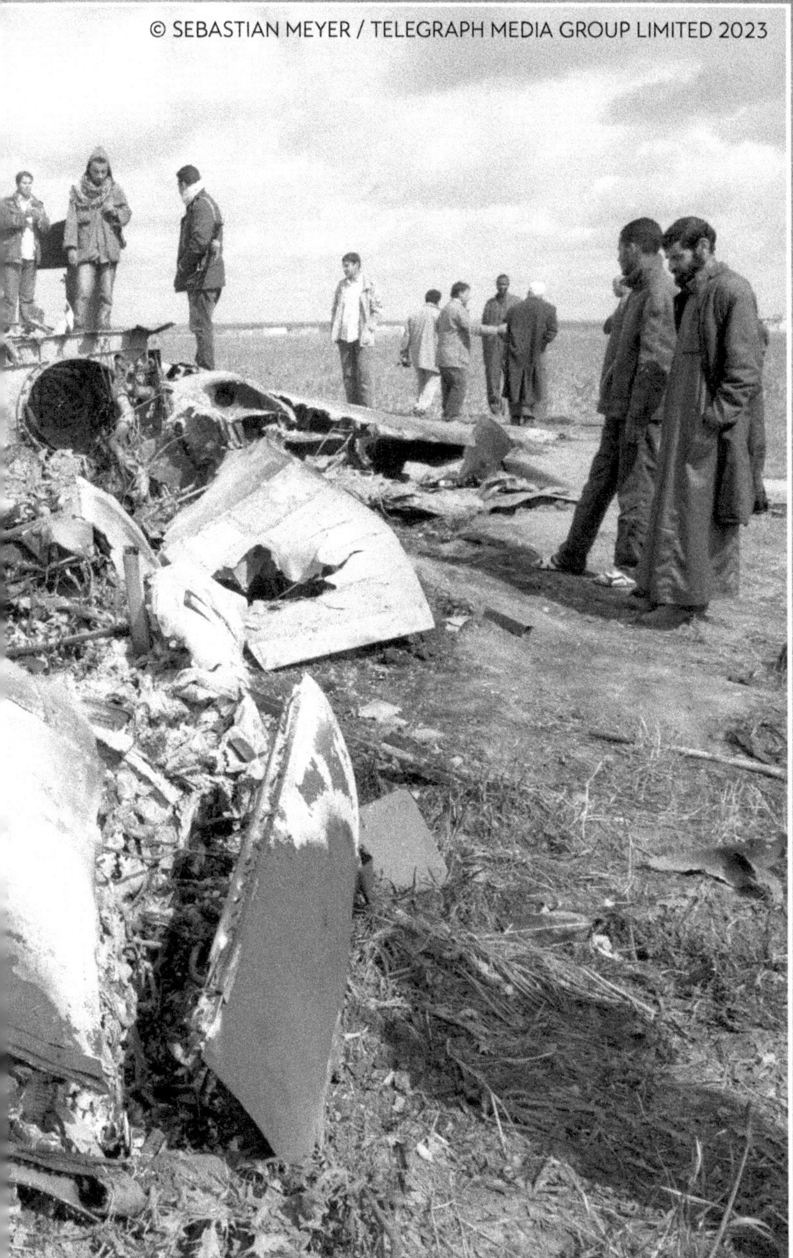

I JUST WANTED TO HEAR FIRSTHAND WHAT SOUNDED LIKE AN INCREDIBLE STORY THAT THE PRESIDENT OF THE UNITED STATES, FOR WHATEVER REASON, REFUSED TO TELL ME WELL. I WANTED TO HEAR ALL ABOUT TYLER STARK'S LIBYAN ADVENTURE.

FOREWORD

by Michael Lewis

Back in the summer of 2012, I was assigned by *Vanity Fair* magazine to profile former President Barack Obama. It wasn't meant to be the usual profile of a sitting president. The idea was to persuade Obama to let me walk in his shoes, to describe what it felt like to play the role he'd been elected to play. I wound up spending six months following Barack Obama around inside the White House, flying with him on foreign trips, playing in his pickup basketball game, and so on. After a while, it became clear that the hardest part of the President's job was the part that the public didn't really see: the quiet moments in which he was required to make some decision. These decisions were almost always unpleasant; any decision that was easy and fun to make got made by some underling. The decisions that reached the President were the ones that were most likely to haunt him for the rest of his life.

When I asked Obama to give me a few examples of unpleasant decisions he'd been forced to make, the first thing he said was "Benghazi." He was referring to his 2011 decision to use the U.S. military to intervene, as Muammar Gadhafi and his troops marched across the country, seemingly intent on wiping out the six hundred thousand residents of Benghazi. In the end, Obama's decision probably prevented a massacre, but, in the moment, he had no idea how it would work out. In the moment, the President knew only that if anything went wrong, the American people would hold him accountable. And sure enough, once the shooting started, something went wrong. An American soldier was lost. Not figuratively lost; not killed in action: literally, lost.

That's when President Obama told me a very brief, and highly unsatisfying, version of the story of a young airman named Tyler Stark. On the first night of bombing, Stark had been forced to eject from his plane over the Libyan desert. For many hours, no one knew what had happened to him. And so there had been a moment, right after the United States commenced its bombing of Gaddafi's forces, when the President realized that the success, or failure, of the mission might turn on what became of Tyler Stark.

A few weeks after the President told me the bad version of the story of Tyler Stark, I found myself in the home of Tyler's parents, asking for a better version. Dorene and Bruce Stark would tell you, I think, that they were a little surprised by my visit, and suspicious of my motives, at least at first. But my motives were pretty straightforward: I just wanted to hear firsthand what sounded like an incredible story that the President of the United States, for whatever reason, refused to tell me well. I wanted to hear all about Tyler Stark's Libyan adventure.

By the time we were finished, I'd heard a lot more than that. The Stark family turned out to have more stories than any six other American families. Some of these stories—like the story of their sons' survival of the Columbine shootings—were terrifying. Others, like the role of faith in their lives, were uplifting. None of them were boring.

In writing about President Obama for *Vanity Fair*, I also wound up writing about Tyler Stark. But after I'd finished writing, I was still left with a pile of unused material on the floor of my office: Stark family stories that I hadn't had room, or reason, to tell. I vaguely recall Dorene saying at the time that she herself might one day tell those stories, but I didn't take her all that seriously. People are always saying they are going to write a book until they sit down and start and realize that, really, they don't want to write a book. But here we are, ten years later, and Dorene Stark has written a book. She has collected all these amazing Stark family stories. They are as powerful and moving as they were when I first heard them.

— MICHAEL LEWIS, journalist

BY LETTING GO,
YOUR "CHALLENGE" BECOMES
AN "ADVENTURE" OF
LEARNING AND GROWTH,
NO LONGER A CHALLENGE
FOR YOU, BUT FOR GOD.

PREFACE

The thought never came to my mind to write a book. I mean, why me? Why a book? It all began on a trip to visit our son who was stationed at the Royal Air Force Base in Lakenheath, England. My bags were packed for our adventure, and I was anxiously awaiting the moment I could capture a hug from our son, who had recently survived an F-15E Strike Eagle plane crash. While making a final check of the contents of my carry-on bag, the thought occured to me to grab a journal. Now, I should reveal to you that I am not one who journals, and I am not typically inclined to document events in my life, but I recognized *the voice* and grabbed a little spiral notebook "just in case." So, from hastily scribbled notes came a documentary of events that would touch and change each one of us in a unique way. Upon our return home, I began sharing the stories of our journey and experiences with family and friends. Repeatedly they told me, "You really should write a book! This is an amazing story!" It was rewarding to see their level of interest, and I so appreciated their feedback, but I really thought they were just extending kindness.

In my heart, I needed to admit it brought me great joy to share the way God had orchestrated so many events in our lives. Sharing not in a boastful way, but rather simply allowing others to see how God continually works for, in, and around us. A way to demonstrate how we often miss His miraculous work simply because we may not be looking.

My hope is to bring awareness to all who are willing to notice that *God is alive* and working on every detail of our lives. Your life (and mine), regardless of faith, religion, or belief system you hold, has a meaning and a purpose for someone, somewhere. It is also my desire to help you take a glance inside your personal world in the joyous times as well as during those challenging times in your life. Perhaps you are in one now. In reality, aren't most of us facing challenges? We all have them. The first question you must ask yourself is: How are you walking through your challenges? "Challenge," as defined by the Cambridge Dictionary, is "something that needs great mental or physical effort in order to be done successfully and therefore tests a person's ability." The second question to ask is: In truth, is it really a challenge, or is it a journey with opportunities to find your inner strength and ability to let go and trust? Perhaps ask yourself how your actions not only affect you yourself, but equally important, how your actions are affecting someone else. Here is the key: You need to focus on the big picture, while "allowing" God to be in charge of the details. He will be your skill and strength. By letting go, your "challenge" becomes an "adventure" of learning and growth, no longer a challenge for you, but for God.

Many of you have experienced events of far greater magnitude and trauma than the ones we have chosen to share. The intent is not to compete with you, only to share with you. The miracles that happen in the daily lives of those whom God has called are happening in every moment of every day, everywhere. Perhaps opening these pages of our family to you will help you, in turn, find hope and see miracles, regardless of the challenges you are facing. Regardless of the outcome you must come to terms with, you are not alone. You are never alone.

―――――― ❧ ――――――

Nevertheless, I am continually with you;
you hold my right hand.

PSALM 73:23 ESV

――――――――――――

My desire in sharing with you is to help provoke and inspire what already exists in your being—the desire to know who you are and to find the relationship you long for between your true self and the Divine. Sometimes these situations are brought into our lives to grow our character and knowledge so that we may be sculpted into the person we were created to be.

A relative, Erin Stark, inquired about Tyler's story. She just so happens to be a long-time designer with TLC Book Design. Erin encouraged me to write the book and offered her assistance in getting me started if, or when, I ever became interested. It took me two years and much prodding from my inner being to finally make that call.

It just so happened that I attended a Women of Faith Conference. The speakers shared many stories, like mine, of how God had been working in their lives and had brought them to this moment, courageously touring the nation to share their hearts. The final speaker's last words were these:

> "Ladies, we have come here to share our stories. Many of you out there have similar stories. If you have a story you have lived through, a story that might make a difference in ONE life, then you have a story that needs to be told. TELL IT! It serves no one to keep it hidden!"

Wow! Those words resonated deep within me. I was sure she was speaking directly to me, though I was only one of eight thousand women there. I *was* holding onto God's story, but why? Quite honestly, the wave of fear and doubt came over me, trying to convince me my story wouldn't measure up. I am not a "professional" writer, author, etc. The list of all the reasons I shouldn't write would grow to be as long as I allowed it. The biggest reason not to write: Would anyone care? There are millions of books out there, would mine really matter? Wouldn't life be less stressful without the worry of it? Why bother? The words of that beautiful speaker continued to return to me: "TELL IT! It serves no one to keep it hidden!" Those words were the confirmation I needed to get going! I finally surrendered—but not without some trepidation.

Shortly after our return home from England, we received a call from Michael Lewis. At the time, Michael was a journalist for *Vanity Fair* magazine as well as the author of numerous books, including *The Blind Side, The Big Short, Moneyball,* and *Liar's Poker*, to name just a few. Michael was in the process of compiling information for *Vanity Fair* regarding President Obama and the challenges that take place in the White House during tumultuous times. At this time, President Obama mentioned the Libya event. Michael was hoping to meet the parents of this airman. And visit he did. It was a brief layover in Denver, Colorado, on his way home from Washington, DC, but such an honor to have spent time with him and answer some of his questions.

As he was leaving, he offered his phone number should we ever need his advice in the future. Five years had now passed since that visit, and I was sure we were the furthest thought from his mind, but I took him up on his offer. I collected some courage, took a deep breath, and picked up my phone, quietly praying that God would disconnect the call if this was not the direction I should be going. Also, I was quietly preparing myself for rejection if he gracefully discouraged the idea. He actually did remember the story and welcomed my call with warmth and understanding. His advice to me was, yet again, more confirmation and encouragement to proceed. "If for no other reason, Dorene, write it for your family." That was all I needed; in fact, it was exactly what I needed. Thank you, Michael. You probably have no idea how those simple words have been an inspiration to me through the entire process.

This conversation was a pivotal point in my decision. Michael conveyed a deep sense of integrity and compassion. I will always be grateful for his generosity of time and his willingness to share his knowledge and expertise.

Where should I begin? The question had barely begun to form in my mind, but I knew exactly where I needed to begin. Right at the source! I would need God's help with this. Again, I am not an author. *God, if this is your will for me, you will need to put together our team, as I have no knowledge on how to bring this together.* I was reminded of Erin's offer and called her. Her voice said it all. "I wondered how long it would take you to finally reach out to me. I am happy to help." She requested notes about the story, which at that time were rough, spotty, and in some cases, not even chronologically correct. I was embarrassed to share them, though I understood she needed to see the story content.

Through contacts, phone calls, and spiritual guidance, she and the Lord put together the perfect team, beginning with Tamara Dever, the owner and founder of TLC Book Design, proofreader Misti Moyer, and our editor, Jennifer Goodson. Jennifer explained early on that she was not interested in taking on a new commitment as her life was already consumed with her family and multiple commitments. Nevertheless, she agreed to pray around this and, to our delight, accepted the task. Coincidence?

Now, with all these people on the team, I realized I had blindly jumped into uncharted territory. This was also an answer to my prayers, as I had no resources to pull from, only the desire to fulfill His will and perhaps my purpose. I felt like He had just put me on assignment! It also felt like a huge undertaking, since I had not a clue as to where to begin. Oh, well . . . here we go!

It's in the letting go His perfect work is done.
Until you say "yes," the gift cannot be opened.

I share this as a reminder. God's plan is not always our plan, and our time is not always His time. However, His *love* can powerfully put the desire in your heart to walk beside Him. *Faith* gives you the courage to *trust*, even when it is uncomfortable.

Your *obedience* completes the triangle. With obedience comes a life with no regrets. How many times have you asked yourself, "What if . . . ?"

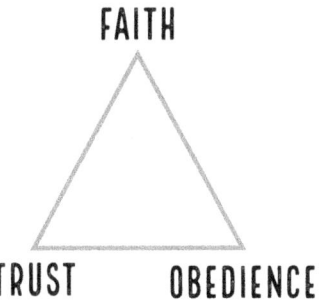

YOU WERE ALL PART OF HIS DIVINE PLAN TO HELP BRING OUT THE BEST IN EACH ONE OF US FOR THE GREATER GOOD. MY DEEPEST GRATITUDE GOES OUT TO ALL OF YOU.

ACKNOWLEDGMENTS

A sincere thank you to my beloved husband of forty-five years. Bruce, your gentle strength and steadfast love inspired me. The encouragement and patience you offered allowed me the freedom to pursue this endeavor. Your trust provided me with a peaceful confidence. Thank you, Trevor and Tyler, for opening the pages of your lives and for your willingness to openly share your hearts. This book is about you and for you and would not have been the same without you.

To my amazing editor, Jennifer Goodson, I so appreciate that you allowed me to use my voice and to speak from my heart. Thank you for staying with me, even thru life's curves!

Erin Stark, this all happened because of you. You added the spark to ignite the flame in my heart. Your kindness and patience provided me a gentle grounding, and the design of my book's interior is gorgeous.

To the founder of TLC Book Design and my cover designer, Tamara Dever, thank you for your willingness to take on this project without hesitation. Your encouragement was always calming. You have an amazing team.

Dr. Ken Kulig, I so appreciate the input and encouraging support you have given. I am thankful for your kindness and your courage in giving a quiet story new life. It brings us a sense of completion we have long desired.

Michael Lewis, you have been such an inspiration to me throughout this process. Your kindness, expertise, thoughtfulness, and time have kept me humbled and grateful. More details on Michael are given in the Preface.

To each one of you in my life that contributed in some way in making this book happen, I am forever grateful. Whether it was sharing your piece of the story, sharing your words of support, or sharing your love and patience with the process, each one of you made a difference. You were all part of His divine plan to help bring out the best in each one of us for the greater good. My deepest gratitude goes out to you.

You know the saying, "It takes a village." To all of you, who are now a part of my village, I am deeply grateful for each of you in my life.

A STORY FOR GOD'S GLORY

———— ⌇ ————

And the grace of our Lord was exceeding abundant with faith and love which is in Christ Jesus.

1 TIMOTHY 1:14 KJV

————————————

My hope is that you will come to know the importance of understanding the difference between *faith* and *trust*. To inspire you to find the ability to truly "let go and let God." To shift your awareness to a more intimate relationship with God and how He empowers us when we do.

God is the author of our life. When we give that life to Him, and completely trust Him with it, we empower Him to do great things *for* us and *in* us—a relationship created in *love* to define our purpose by *divine design*.

Think about the word *trust* and what it really means to "let go and let God," with the complete belief that *He will* take care of every detail. One of the lessons taught to me when I asked God about faith was the difference between faith and trust and that you can have one without the other. Let me explain. Faith is defined by Webster as a "firm belief in something for which there is no proof. Something that is believed especially with strong conviction." You believe in the existence.

Trust is defined by *Merriam-Webster* as a "firm belief in the reliability, truth, and strength of someone or something (confidence, certainty, and assurance)." You believe in the power. Obedience puts this faith and trust into action.

We can have faith, believe there is a God, and yet still lack trust in His faithfulness to us. However, it is your obedience to *His will,* with faith and trust in place that truly begins the relationship between you and the Divine. This is where the spiritual communion begins to form and manifest itself inside of you. As it is written in Matthew 6:30-34, the Lord explains that we need to seek Him and His righteousness first. We also need to trust Him with *all* of our needs.

With this in mind, let us share the story of one military family and see how God can prevail in the midst of many storms when we step aside and allow Him to do His work.

Freedom and Family

Freedom comes at an extraordinary price. It is not free, and it is not fair. Many innocent lives are sacrificed for the choices, lifestyles, and prosperity that are currently available to us. For many military families, the outcome of this sacrifice is devastating. Often it leaves these families without the ability to overcome its wrath. Things could have easily turned out much different for our family as well.

My husband Bruce and I have shared forty-five years of marriage and the joy of raising our two sons, Trevor and Tyler. Trevor, the older of the two, is married to Bree, and together they have two lovely children, a girl and a boy. Trevor's heart's desire as a young boy was not only to become a father but also to find his unique way to give back to humanity. Isn't it just like God to put those desires in our hearts so we may follow His purpose for us? Trevor currently enjoys a career as a leadership consultant with Spectrum and lives a successful life filled with the blessings of a wonderful family and career.

Tyler is the younger brother and is married to Kelly; they have twin boys. At the initial writing of this book, Tyler has been in the military for fourteen years. His first assignment was to Lakenheath, England, in 2006. His rank is Lt. Col., Chief of Advanced Training Division, AFCENT Air Warfare Center, located in the United Arab Emirates, where Tyler and his family reside in Abu Dhabi. Tyler is a WSO for the United States Air Force, training navigators in F-15E Strike Eagles.

As a family, some of our fondest memories have been our travels together. It might have been as simple as a long weekend tent camping in the Colorado Rockies, or a road trip through the United States, or plane adventures out of the country. It was the escape from schedules and duties in exchange for time spent sharing and just being together that brought us such joy and deeper relationships.

To all families everywhere, we are all in this together. All of us come with our many challenges, as well as with our many blessings and miracles. We travel through our own existence, often searching for our purpose. My hope is our stories will help you discover how intimate God is and how He is working in your life in every moment of your day. When He says He'll never leave you, it's a promise. It is *real*. When you feel division or separation, it is your own stepping away, not His.

"Be strong and courageous.
Do not be afraid or terrified because of them,
for the LORD your God goes with you;
he will never leave you nor forsake you."

DEUTERONOMY 31:6

Do you recognize God's love?

Because it is in Jesus, and Jesus lives within you. His love now becomes yours, to be nurtured and shared. You now have the same Spirit. We are all connected with the same Spirit. What a gift of grace!

Do you recognize your purpose? It is only to love Him in return. The molding of the clay is entirely His handiwork. He will make you His masterpiece.

For we are God's masterpiece.
He has created us anew in Christ Jesus, so we can do
the good things he planned for us long ago.
EPHESIANS 2:10 NLT

The adventure begins when you can awaken your eyes and ignite your inner spirit, so you may witness God's glory in the smallest moments of your days, as well as the details in every miracle He gives. Perhaps the accounts shared here will give you a human experience to the expression "let go and let God." *Allow yourself the freedom to just be.*

Yes, He is the author of everyone's story. This is ours.

• • •

Our story is told with many contributors throughout the book. Please make note of graphic lines (like the one below) placed between sections.

TYLER

These are cues of another's experience within our story.

"FROM SIX CALAMITIES HE WILL RESCUE YOU;
IN SEVEN NO HARM WILL TOUCH YOU."

JOB 5:19

———————————

God did this for my son, Tyler.
This is our story.

LIFE IS NOT VOID OF ITS TWISTS AND TURNS AND MANY CHALLENGES, EVEN WHEN YOU ARE FOLLOWING YOUR PATH. THOSE ARE THE EXACT EVENTS THAT GIVE US THE CHARACTER WE NEED TO PROCEED.

chapter one

BAILOUT!

Even after his parachute opened, Tyler Stark sensed he was coming down too fast. The last thing he'd heard was the pilot saying, "Bailout! Bailout! Bail—" Before the third call was finished, there'd come the violent kick in the rear from the ejector seat, then a rush of cool air. They called it "opening shock" for a reason. He was disoriented. A minute earlier, when the plane had started to spin—it felt like a car hitting a patch of ice—his first thought had been that everything was going to be fine: My first mission, I had my first close call. He'd since changed his mind. He could see the red light of his jet's rocket fading away and also, falling more slowly, the pilot's parachute. He went immediately to his checklist: he untangled himself from his life raft, then checked the canopy of his chute and saw the gash. That's why he was coming down too fast. How fast he couldn't say, but he told himself he'd have to execute a perfect landing. It was the middle of the night. The sky was black. Below his feet he could see a few lights and houses, but mainly it was just desert. . . .

1

Even so, as he floated down, he felt almost calm. The night air was cool, and there was no sound, only awesome silence. He didn't really know why he'd been sent here, to Libya, in the first place. He knew his assignment, his specific mission. But he didn't know the reason for it. He'd never met a Libyan. Drifting high over the desert he had no sense that he was at once an expression of an idea framed late one night in the White House by the president himself, writing with a No. 2 pencil, and also, suddenly, a threat to that idea. He didn't sense these invisible threads in his existence, only the visible ones yoking him to his torn parachute. His thoughts were only of survival. He realized, If I can see my plane exploding, and my chute in the air, so can the enemy. He'd just turned 27—one of the only three facts about himself, along with his name and rank, that he was now prepared to divulge if captured.

He scanned the earth beneath his dangling feet. He was going to hit hard, and there was nothing he could do about it.[1]

— MICHAEL LEWIS, journalist
Vanity Fair, October 2012 issue

---

[1] Michael Lewis, "Obama's Way," *Vanity Fair, September 11, 2012, www.vanityfair.com/news/2012/10/michael-lewis-profile-barack-obama.*

TYLER

It all began on March 17, 2011. It was a Thursday. Walking into scheduling at 07:00 at RAF Lakenheath, I never thought my life was about to change. There had been a lot of weather issues early in the week, leading to many canceled flights. It was my job to be the duty scheduler that day, so I went in to begin reflowing the schedule for the rest of the week. Upon beginning, I saw that all flights had been canceled for the day, and I assumed it was due to bad weather. This type of decision is usually made at the last possible moment in the event the weather clears. Which, in turn, means you are usually preparing, planning, and briefing for a flight with little chance of taking off.

However, as others began to show up for duty, it became apparent flights *had not* been canceled due to weather. Something else was going on. At this time, a message was put on the screen at the OPS desk that there was a meeting in the main auditorium (large enough to seat four hundred people) at 08:00. Still no word of what actually was going on, and it seemed we would not find out until 08:00.

• • •

Joining the Military

Why did I want to join the military? As a young boy, I had a love for airplanes and was fascinated by the notion that one day, I could have the ability and the experience to soar

3

through the air, flying like a bird, in a sky that appeared limitless to me. At the young age of two, I expressed my desire to be a pilot one day to my parents. Well, like any parent of a two-year-old, my parents were very supportive. Honestly, how many children at that age do not have a fascination with becoming a pilot, fireman, or trash collector? They didn't take me too seriously but never discounted my dream. At the age of five, my parents took me to the Air Force Academy with some visiting cousins. Unknowingly, it happened to be the week before graduation ceremonies, so they were practicing the flyover. As I took it all in, with eyes a-glow in wonder and sheer imagination, as those planes thundered overhead, I made my declaration. "Hey, Mom and Dad! When I become a pilot, I am going to fly one of those!"

According to them, my conviction that day seemed so strong, they didn't doubt the possibility. Since that moment, my entire family and extended family encouraged me and supported me even to this day. Of course, as a youngster, I never let go of that dream even though I didn't know how to accomplish it, but I knew I wanted to be in the air. I was also looking at the excitement side of it all, wearing that stately looking uniform and traveling to cities all over the world. Honestly, it appealed to my ego as well.

My family had taken many vacations over the years, which certainly gave me the taste of an exciting life as a pilot. (Not to mention the stewardesses!) That was

"Hey, Mom and Dad! When I become a pilot I'm going to fly one of those!"

Tyler and Trevor at the Academy with cousins, Mark and Tara Thomsen.

Early cockpit training. Who knew?

my perception growing up. The dream and desire stayed with me during my teen years and even through college.

In summary, I came up with two different routes to becoming a pilot. One road would take me there privately; this can be quite costly, as the hourly requirements are extensive and the pay scale quite lacking in the beginning. Starting with small Cessnas and working your way into commercial planes can also require a long timeline.

The second choice is the military avenue, which is a tradeoff. This is "free" training to be qualified as a pilot, but at the same time, you are not guaranteed a pilot slot, and you have invested a lot of time and commitment. Obviously, as far as my pure and naive rationale, I was going to have to look at things a bit more realistically.

After 9/11, motivation of simply living the enchanted life of a pilot had now changed into a desire to serve my country and to "take the fight back" to those who had made an attack on the United States. I still had the desire to join the Air Force and to become a pilot, but now, I had a much greater sense of patriotism while still chasing my dreams. This aligned quite nicely to my way of thinking. However, I still had not done enough research. I spoke with a recruiter on the enlisted side. My grandfather had wanted me to join the Navy, but upon checking, it was clear the Air Force was a better option due to lower numbers of jets in the Navy and the lower availability of pilot slots. Clearly, my best option would be the Air Force. At this point, I knew I needed to figure out for certain what type of military plane I wanted to fly, while keeping my dream of flying of fighter jets in the back of my mind.

You're probably familiar with the movie *Top Gun*. I watched it repeatedly and absolutely loved it! Couldn't get enough of it! (Little did I know then how this movie would play out in my own life.) I decided this was what I wanted to do. If I was going to fly, then I was going to fly a fighter because that's the best! That's the pinnacle! I wanted to fly for the United States Air Force—the best fighting force in the world! Not only to become a pilot to fulfill my dreams, but to travel the world and serve my country. What was once a distant dream was becoming within arms' reach.

As a junior in high school and thinking about college plans, I wanted to go to the Air Force Academy in Colorado, but at the same time, selfishly, I did not want to miss out on the excitement of a more-typical college life. My brother, Trevor, was already in college and had shared some of the social culture with me, which completely drew me in. I wanted to be a part of that. So, going to college for a year and then enlisting in the Air Force sounded like the perfect plan.

Again, not having done enough research, I was unaware an enlisted person is not even able to fly, so this certainly would not have met my goals whatsoever!

I thank the Reserve Officer Training Corps (ROTC) instructor at our freshman orientation who finally clued me in to the fact you must be an officer to fly in the Air Force. So, after hearing about the ROTC program, it sounded just perfect! I go to school, have a terrific college experience, and get to have a taste of the military for a year before signing on the dotted line, and maybe even get the chance to fly. Even then, it was not a guarantee I would get a pilot slot. I still had to be the best, prove myself, and get selected. I thought if you wanted to give flying a try, you could go through the training, which would determine whether you would stay in or not. Contrarily, I learned you must first sign up, be selected, then train to be a pilot. So, I tried out ROTC, enjoyed the culture of the military, and ended up signing for three years with a scholarship, which committed me to the Air Force for an additional four years after graduating college.

I will never forget the day. It was my junior year at Colorado State University, and my selection was coming up, so I would be able to find out what I would be doing in the Air Force: pilot, navigator, intelligence officer, manning personnel officer, etc. You just don't know. You put in your choices, and then you take a series of tests. One is an eye/hand coordination test called the BAT (Basic Aptitude Test), another is the ASVAB (Armed Services Vocational Aptitude Battery), which, fortunately, I scored well in.

What I didn't know, and what could have helped my chances a bit more (in case any of you need this information), was that they include civilian flight time as part of the scoring. Even twenty-five to fifty hours of civilian flight time helps your overall score when you are going up for a flying position. I had none. I knew it was competitive, but I also knew it was not a sure thing. While at home between classes, I received a call from the ROTC secretary, notifying me that I needed to come in and sign some paperwork. I went in and dutifully signed the papers, at which time the colonel informed me I was going to be awarded the Daedalian Scholarship in addition to the ROTC Scholarship, which was awarded for good grades or high performance. He said, "You are going to get the Daedalian Scholarship this semester, which is three thousand dollars."

At the time, I didn't fully understand what this meant, but it sounded awesome! I was also told that even though a pilot slot could not be promised at this moment, the award was given only to pilots. So, reading between the lines, that meant that I had received a pilot slot and a scholarship! My dream job and a bonus on top of it! Could life get any better than that? Things were looking great! I was on top of the world. I needed to return to class though, so I hopped on my motorcycle and headed out. On my way to class, I approached an intersection to make a left turn and was sideswiped by a car. Nothing too serious, but I did get banged up a bit. Fortunately, I had protective gear on, so it was relatively mild for a motorcycle accident. I called my friend Dave and asked if he could bring over his truck to haul the bike back to the house.

As I was sitting on the side of the road, nursing my wounds and talking to the police, my phone rang. Too busy to answer at that moment, I let the phone go to voicemail. Once I had calmed down and gotten things back on track, I listened to the message. "There has been a clerical error, and you are not qualified to get the Daedalian Scholarship. Your eyesight is right on the limit and does not meet our requirements." This was truly a day of highs and lows. At that time, it was my understanding the military did not allow Lasik or PRK surgery. What I didn't know, being so new to the military, was that those rules had changed, and if I had undergone the surgery ahead of time, I could have had the pilot slot I had worked so hard to earn and felt like I deserved.

So, I went from sitting on top of the world, with all my dreams ahead of me and feeling invincible, to sitting on the side of the road with a bruised-up body, a banged-up motorcycle, and news that I had lost my pilot slot just hours after receiving it. My bruised-up body now included a broken heart. It had surely been an emotional roller-coaster kind of day. I would be willing to bet that most of you have experienced a day like that, where you wonder why you got out of bed. You can understand my devastation as a twenty-two-year-old.

———— ✑ ————

Life is not void of its twists and turns and many challenges, even when you are following your path. Those are the exact events that give us the character we need to proceed.

The next afternoon, I went in to see the commander. He could see I was clearly disappointed and apologized, saying, "Do you know how to swim?"

"Yes," I replied.

"Do you like to swim?"

"Sure."

"Well, would you like to go to Pensacola, where you will become a Weapons Systems Officer (WSO)? Your options are navigating an F-15E fighter or a B1 bomber."

These are pretty good options and guaranteed me a seat in a fighter jet if I continued to perform well, versus a pilot slot with no guarantees on which plane I would be assigned to. This felt like a pretty decent offer, so that is what I did. I finished college, got my commissioning, and started my training in Pensacola with the Navy.

Interesting, to say the least, when one reflects on the sequence of events. In my mind, do I wish I had done the research on the vision requirements prior, or was it possible the information was not presented to me because, in fact, this was the perfect plan for me? This is where we often question God and/or second-guess ourselves and regret our choices. Perhaps we should simply surrender, believing we are exactly where we are supposed to be to fulfill our life purpose.

———————⚮———————

*God has already arranged a comeback for every
setback, a vindication for every wrong,
a new beginning for every disappointment.*

JOEL OSTEEN

———————————————————

REFLECTION

Reflect for a moment about God filling the desires of our hearts. The seed was planted years ago, and through the years, it has been watered and nurtured. The process begins when we become open to the awareness of the gifts within us. We've all been given the ability to touch a life. When you see it, identify with it. When you see it in another person, help them identify it by helping their awareness process. Claim it . . . own it . . . and nurture it. These gifts and desires can help guide us to the person we were created to be.

*Take delight in the LORD, and he will give you
the desires of your heart.*

PSALM 37:4

chapter two

A CHANGE OF COURSE

⸻ ∽ ⸻

But let all who take refuge in you be glad;
let them ever sing for joy.
Spread your protection over them, that those
who love your name may rejoice in you.

PSALM 5:11

DORENE

Our story begins in the spring of 2011. Tyler is now a captain in the Air Force and has been stationed at the Royal Air Force Base in Lakenheath, England, for about seven months. As parents, we, of course, had a longing to spend time with our son and had talked about visiting the United Kingdom for years. What better reason to incorporate a long-awaited visit to the UK? Our travel plans had already been completed. We were to travel with our friends, Mike and Paula, and were going to meet Tyler's new friend, Kelly. Our plans included time touring London, Lakenheath Air Force Base, the town of Bath, and the surrounding areas. Our trip dates were March 25 through April 2. These dates were aligned to spring break schedule with our school system. This is important to note, because God's timing is *always* perfect. Never early, never late, just right on time. Little did we know what lay ahead of us. Reservations were made for plane fares, car rental, hotels, and several quaint bed and breakfasts along the way. Our excitement was beginning to build as the time drew near.

TYLER

I was now in the auditorium, filled with both F-15E squadrons and both squadrons' operational personnel, in addition to key maintainers and leadership. At the briefing, we found out the conflict in Libya had escalated. We were being directed to fly strike missions initially from RAF Lakenheath and then from Aviano AB, Italy. We initially received an intelligence update on the situation, followed by a SERE (survival, evasion, resistance, and escape) brief on the terrain and evading options in Libya. Included in the briefs was an EPA (evade plan of action), which highlights which areas are preferable to eject if you have to, which areas you want to avoid, not only for ease of survival but evasion from the enemy, and overall expected support from locals. Due to the majority of the country being loyal to Muammar Gaddafi at the time, excluding the rebels in Benghazi, the recommendation was to eject over water to facilitate a quick pick-up from the Navy, which was located just off the coast. If ejection had to be made over land, it was *very* undesirable, but the safest place was around 600 nautical miles south of the coast.

Teamwork from all the squadrons was a must if we were going to have a successful mission, especially with such short notice. Following the briefing, each crew member had duties they were to accomplish during the Mission Planning Cell (MPC) over the next twelve hours, at which time a new crew would man the MPC. Both squadrons would start twenty-four-hour operations and establish a battle rhythm. Names began to be assigned and displayed with each assigned duty posting which crews would actually be flying. All assigned pilots were to get a jump start on their twelve hours of crew rest as it was a twelve-jet strike package leaving that night and recovering in Aviano, with another twelve jets to follow the next day.

Following the briefing the energy was high in the room because, except for a few senior people, no one had experienced such a short notice tasking so many jets— twenty-four in all. Though unfamiliar to many, it was not new for the base itself. In the 1980s, the 494th had been given a similar task, operation El Dorado Canyon, though with considerably more time—on the order of weeks—to plan. This mission was also similar in objectives: go to Libya and strike Muammar Gaddafi, this time in retaliation for the Iran bombing in the 1980s. The buzz in the room was this operation was El Dorado Canyon, Take II.

Though a younger member of the squadron, I was disappointed, but not surprised, to not see my name on any of the lists. My role was to provide support to scheduling and the mobility shop to get the guys out the door. It also kept my options open to fly as I had not been tagged with MPC duties. Midway through Thursday it was clear the combatant commander for AFRICOM was not going to give us the green light for strikes that night. We did not know when the word would come, so we continued to plan and prepare.

I showed up Friday morning to the updated duties board posting to see if I was now in the line to fly a jet that night. It's the same as walking into a locker room and finding out you are going to be a starter for the big game. I was really excited. The battle rhythm was 12:00 to 00:00 and 00:00 to 12:00, so I had a few hours to get an intel update and look at the productions the MPC had generated before I had to go home for crew rest. The operation was classified at that time, so I could not tell my family or my girlfriend, Kelly, what was going on or that I might be deploying that night.

That afternoon, we were told we still did not have a green light from the general and so we waited at home to have crew rest for whenever they needed us. So, we were in limbo through Friday and Saturday afternoon waiting for the phone to ring. When it did, we were notified to come in immediately for a briefing. No other information was given to us. We arrived at 13:00 and were told takeoffs had slipped; we might take off at 17:00 or as late as 19:00. In the meantime, we continued to familiarize ourselves with the mission tactics and information, including rules of engagement, special theater instructions (which were only in draft form at the time), country layout, and updates on Gaddafi forces. Also, I needed to review and confirm my ISOPREP.

An ISOPREP is a document used if you eject and are forced to evade. It contains your physical characteristics as well as three personal statements that can be used to authenticate you by friendly forces upon your pickup. Everything looked as I remembered it.

At around 19:00, we were told we were flying, not executing a strike mission. Due to delays at the CAOC (Combined Air Operations Center), strike missions were currently on hold, although they still needed jets with bombs ferried to Aviano so they would be ready for sustained combat operations. Not what I had psyched myself up for, but I was still in the fight and getting closer to my first combat sortie.

With this new change in plans, I sent a quick email to my parents who were traveling to the UK to see me the next week.

March 3/18/11 – Just curious . . . Did you get trip insurance? . . .

DORENE

Bruce and I couldn't help but wonder why he would ask, but indeed, we had purchased it. Then came another email from Tyler on March 20, 2011, saying:

> Just so you guys know, I am no longer in the UK. I can't tell you where I am, but the problem is, I don't know when I will be back. I will try to be back for your trip, but it's unknown at this time. Mom and Dad, you are welcome to come and visit England as planned. Kelly, if you are okay with it, you can show them around. Love you. Talk to you soon. – Tyler

Though there was nothing too alarming in this email, other than a slight change in plans, I began to experience an intense and very familiar sensation in my stomach. I had to ask myself, "*why?*" I pondered it for a short time, thinking the military had made a schedule change and didn't honor Tyler's leave request. I started out just a bit annoyed, until my stomach began turning inside out, which immediately sends out a red flag warning for me! *Now, I can't ignore that familiar pit in my stomach!*

TYLER

We landed after midnight as we were the first four-ship to land in Aviano. An ADVON team had gone to Aviano the day prior to our departure, and I was expecting things to be somewhat setup. However, I was soon to find out that wasn't the case. By the time we in-processed to the base and got to the hanger, we began operations at 01:30. The ADVON team needed help and the lt. colonel, who was the DO for the 492nd and had already been up for well over thirty hours, started querying everyone he didn't know on what their "at home jobs" were. As soon as I told him I was a scheduler, he told me, "Start building a flying schedule and set a battle rhythm, starting at 04:00. Pair experienced people with inexperienced people." That was it. Then he left.

Needless to say, I felt I was in over my head, even if for just a moment. I had only been a scheduler for a couple of weeks and was still very much learning the ropes. *I didn't even know what a battle rhythm was!* Not to mention the fact no one was quite sure how many jets were coming in . . . or what time . . . or who was on them . . . due to communications still being set up. Talk about a heavy task! This made creating a flying schedule rather difficult to say the least. But as the morning progressed, people began showing up at the squadron, and I got names, experience level, and crew position. By 07:00 that morning, I had a 90-percent solution for the next day. By the time I went to bed, I had been up twenty-seven hours and had to be back in the squadron at 14:00 to schedule the following day.

As the duty scheduler for the day, I made sure I was scheduled for one of the first flights as I was excited for my first combat mission. The next day, I met Major Kenneth "MeSo" Harney, the pilot I would fly beside.

I recognized him but didn't really know him. He was previously in combat in Afghanistan as a WSO and as a pilot. He was well experienced. This put me at ease to know I (also a WSO) was going to be flying with someone who had seen combat multiple times, unlike myself.

My shift was scheduled to end at 02:00, but I had to leave at 00:45 for crew rest for the following night. Due to the irregular times I had been going to bed and the buzz of the initial setup of the squadron, I was tired but couldn't fall asleep. So, I took a no-go pill (Ambien) to make sure I was rested for the flight later that day. I woke up after nine hours of sleep feeling rested, grabbed some local food on base, and headed in.

Due to the secrecy of the combat operations at the time, we would wear green flight suits into work and then change into desert flight suits, which were an indicator you were flying combat missions. There were few desert flight suits to go around, and I had to fight with the logistics readiness squadron just to get the one I had, which was a little too big. I didn't even have time to sew rank on the uniform or velcro for our patches, and the boots were "close enough" to my size but also a little big. The first time I even wore them was when I was changing into all the desert gear. So, for my first combat mission, I was dressed in an oversized flight suit and boots, with incorrect identity patches on my suit.

Once changed and ready, I headed to the intel brief. With no troops on the ground and extremely early in the campaign, the picture of where Gaddafi's forces were and where the rebels were was very muddled, with no definitive line. I reviewed my ISOPREP one more time, *not recognizing the wrong survival radio was listed*, and headed right into our flight brief. Normally, when flying in combat, you have a mission passed to you via an ATO (Air Tasking Order), describing where you are going, who you will be talking to and on what frequency, when and where your tanker will be, and the overall intent of the mission. But we did not have that luxury. Our ATO had not been published. We had very little information on what we were to accomplish on this mission. All we knew was we were to fly to Libya, check in, and await a tasking.

Though not the standard, we were well trained for dynamic missions like this. Due to not receiving our tasking yet, the flight brief was relatively quick. This was fine because there were a number of other things to check on this specific flight, than on a normal training mission. Unique to this flight versus training, we had a combat survival vest. I knew what was in it, but there was no time to review where things were kept, which unbeknownst to me would play a factor later. We were also given a 9mm handgun as well as our NVGs (night vision goggles). The whole preparation prior to actually stepping onto the jet was familiar, but not as practiced. Many things you can't or don't have time to simulate in training suddenly become real and require attention. What seemed familiar had more reality to it now.

In the hustle to get out of Lakenheath, I had left my flashlight in my flight locker. The life support pallets with the flashlights had not yet arrived. So, as we were leaving the building and the crews were coming back in from their flight in Libya, I asked my buddy "Boozer" if I could borrow his, promising to give it back as soon as we got back. We got issued our "go" pills (dextroamphetamine) in case our mission got extended. We got our tail numbers, an airfield update, and stepped to our jets for an inspection walk-around and checklist.

On the way out, we could see one crew coming back. They were only the second formation of Strike Eagles that had been in Libya. Due to extended taskings and limited airborne gas, the first crew flew from Lakenheath the night prior and had to divert into Malta. The implication of this was, although we were the third formation going in, we had not talked to anyone who was there to pass on their lessons learned and what to expect. So, we were going in just as blind from an aircrew perspective as the first formation.

Since we were only the second formation leaving from Aviano, even getting to our jets was confusing. We also lost time while navigating the unfamiliar base and ramp area that now had increased security. We did a normal walkaround assessment, but this was the first time I had seen a live bomb with all the arming wires. MeSo followed behind me to verify I didn't miss anything. The jet and ordinance were all good to go, so we hopped in and started it up.

We took off at 17:00, which was normal, and we started our two-hour flight down to Libya. On the way, MeSo gave me some pointers on what to expect, and I familiarized myself with the Smart Pack (a quick reference to theatre specific requirements and information), and most important, where the radio frequencies were. Unlike in training, when they tell you to contact your tanker on 336.1, they tell you to push to a TOD, like Beige 71 or Green 43. There is a table with eight or nine colors and different numbers, and you have to find the frequency. Thankfully, MeSo filled me in on this because we never really talked about it and never practiced it in training. It is one of those many small things which are different in combat that can make you feel like you are "behind the jet" and playing catch up. We also ensured that every aspect of all our systems was working properly.

As we approached Southern Italy, we checked in with ATC and asked about the status of a fuel tanker. We noticed there was an aircraft flying parallel to us. The controller directed us to Exxon 06, which was a fuel tanker of opportunity since our planned tanker had maintenance issues and never took off. As we checked into the AOR (Area of Responsibility), the radio plan got a little tough for me to follow. We transitioned to several radios to a secure frequency, only to find our secure radio capability in the jet was not functioning, though it had been working prior to take-off.

By this point in the flight, MeSo and I had established a good understanding of our crew coordination and began to efficiently operate as a crew ready for combat. So, I started working to get the secure radio back up while he followed along the tanker plan. All of the tasking and any target-related communications have to be done on a secure radio. Without a secure radio working we were severely limited in our capability to obtain targets and drop bombs on them.

Regardless of all the checklists, once airborne, things can still go wrong. Due to threats in the area, our tankers were more than 150 miles from the AOR, so it gave me some time to troubleshoot the radios and eventually get the secure radio working as we checked back in on the command and control frequency after getting topped-up with gas. I get us back up on secure radio to hear the tail end of our tasking. While transiting from the tankers to the AOR, you could see ADA (Air Defense Artillery) at our altitude. Though it was not a factor for us, it made me realize everything was definitely real. This was definitely not training!

chapter three

BLANKET OF PROTECTION

He who dwells in the secret place of the Most High
Shall abide under the shadow of the Almighty.
I will say of the LORD, "He is my refuge
and my fortress; My God, in Him I will trust."

PSALM 91:1-2

DORENE

Upon reading Tyler's email, as a mother, I began to have that intuitive sense we mothers feel when our child might be in harm's way. We don't need an explanation. It is just there. Call it a mother's sixth sense, or perhaps innate wisdom. I had experienced it before if my children were in a bad or dangerous situation or perhaps with some friends who might be a bad influence. It has always served me well, and I have learned to always *listen* to it and to always *trust* it.

I am not a fearful person, nor is worrying a part of my life. However, I know from past experiences this is my warning from God when things are not going so well. I had no other information, just a sense of urgency. I immediately went into maternal mode, and I knew the first and highest priority was to send out a mass email to our amazing family and friends, to please pray.

On Mar. 20, 2011, at 3:39 PM, Dorene Stark wrote:

Hello everyone,

Calling out to all of you wonderful prayer warriors again. Tyler informed us today he is no longer in London. He is out flying a mission of which he cannot disclose his destination. Given the current situation in Libya, one could suspect it is a likely possibility. We were to leave this Friday (3/25) with Mike and Paula Weaver, to spend spring break with him and his friend, Kelly, in London. However, it looks like that plan may be tabled.

At this point, we have no way of knowing how long his mission will take, so in the meantime, your prayers for his safety and well-being are always appreciated.

Thank you for the blanket of protection that your prayers provide. God Bless each and every one of you—and we will keep you posted.

Love, Dorene and Bruce

I felt this would be an odd email for those on the receiving end with very little information. I held in a deep breath and hit the "send" button. I quickly felt a little bit of relief, knowing God can do great things through the power of prayer. Our prayer warriors are amazing. They have been there for our family on numerous occasions.

As I pushed my chair away from my computer, I was still feeling very unsettled. I sensed a very clear message things were not good, and my duties as a mother were certainly *not* finished.

A sweet and gentle voice came into my thoughts. *There is more to do. The prayer is not enough.* I wondered, *what more could there possibly be? The prayer warriors would provide a blanket of protection.* This is what I had always been taught. There is power in prayer. God can give us miracles through prayer! *How is it then that this is not enough?* My mind was spinning with related questions. I was completely perplexed.

There is indeed, one more thing. If a *blanket of prayer* is not enough, there is only one thing greater! That gentle voice was speaking to me again. *My daughter, you must give him back from whence he came. You must give him back to his Father, and now is the time.* The clarity of the request was not to be questioned. I must give my child back to his Maker, his Creator. The reality of this and the intense feeling that came with it stopped me in my tracks. I immediately sat back down, took a deep breath, and focused on the heavenly request that had just been handed to me.

Perhaps you could liken it to the biblical story of Hannah in Samuel I. Hannah pleaded to God for a son, as she was barren, and promised to give him back to God for His exclusive use. When she gave birth to Samuel, as promised, she gave him back, and God surely did use Samuel in His work for the kingdom. In addition, she was blessed with five more children. As mothers, we desire the best for our children. However, in today's society, there is the mixture of good and evil. Thus, our trust in God is put to the test. But if we learn to be like Hannah, we give God charge over our children, and He will protect them in the guiding process. Yes, for mothers, it is a place of fear, but doesn't God's perfect love cast out fear? It's in the *trusting* we embrace His love for us and our children. It's in the *trusting* we can be free of fear and worry. No, it is not easy, but it is why it's called a *relationship*.

It is in the obedience that our faith and trust are nourished and our relationship with God deepens. The obedience is what puts God's work into action. We always have a choice.

DORENE STARK

I, of course, had questions. I had to ask God, "What does that look like in current times? How would I give a living child back to God? What would God find acceptable?" The stakes were high—I wanted it to be perfect in God's eyes, without questioning whether I had done all that was asked of me. I knew in the depth of my being our son's life was at stake. There was no room for error.

As the story unfolds the answers to these questions, you will hopefully see how obedience and faith can literally change the course of a life. It can and I believe it did!

So, I closed my eyes and, once again, asked God to show me. He did, just as He has promised.

"Ask, and you shall receive."

LUKE 11:9

He then gave me the vision of the mountain where our Christ was crucified. Three crosses, but only Christ remaining. He then visually walked me through it. Wrapping up our infant child in swaddling clothes, I carried him toward the cross and gently laid him down at the foot of the cross. In doing so, I recalled the story of Isaac. His father, Abraham, was asked to bring his son, Isaac, to the altar for a sacrifice (Genesis 22:1-18). Without knowing the outcome, Abraham was obedient and brought Isaac to the altar to be burned as a living sacrifice. However, God's angel stepped in and stopped Abraham, preserving the life of his child, Isaac. It was such an example of *love, faith, trust,* and *obedience.* This

29

is what opens our hearts to recognize and receive God's precious blessings.

After running through this biblical event in my mind, I began to have another conversation with God. It sounded like this: *God, you gave me the gift of a miracle in this child's birth twenty-seven years ago. You asked me then to give him back to you, which I did. For twenty-seven years we have been blessed with his life. Now you are asking the same of me again?*

The Foot of the Cross

Do not be anxious about anything,
but in every situation, by prayer and petition,
with thanksgiving, present your requests to God.

PHILIPPIANS 4:6

Do you love me enough, do you trust me enough, do you believe in me enough, to give him back to me? These questions were for my benefit; as you see, He already knew my heart. I was overcome with an amazing sensation. One that words cannot describe. God had my undivided attention! Then came a knowingness, a peace, a gentleness, an unwavering confidence that the absolute perfect place for our son to be was with his heavenly Father. How could I possibly help Tyler with no knowledge of his location or his needs? I was filled with gratitude for the time we were all allowed to share in his young life.

The vision continued of our infant son cradled in my arms. I was ready to lay him at the foot of the cross, with so many thoughts and emotions tugging at my spirit. In this moment, it was made very clear to me, that as I laid our child at the feet of Jesus and said, "Thank you for the years you gave us. We love you little one," that I was not permitted to put any conditions on the outcome of the current situation. I knew that I must completely and entirely surrender to God's will, regardless of the outcome. I also knew in my heart that I was agreeing to the reality that the short and simple email we had received from Tyler might be the last communication we would ever receive from him. I knew I was agreeing to the possibility that we might never hold him, lay eyes on him, or hear his voice or his laughter again. To *trust*, we must fully *surrender*. Yes, fully surrender! This means you don't take back *any* pieces of the control. This also means you now have no reason to worry. What? No worry? You hope I am kidding, right? Worry is not of God; it is from the one who comes to steal your joy. If you are still worried, you have not fully surrendered. It is a great gauge in the learning process. This is where you begin to live in the freedom of trust.

I knew now that I had fulfilled the desires of *His* heart and *His* request. The *blanket of protection* had now been completed, which allowed me to rest in *His* arms.

Of course, we were not sure how things would unfold, so we patiently sat back and waited. Waiting for what, we had no idea. Trying to carry on as normal, without a mention of it to anyone, left us beautifully entwined with the Spirit close to our hearts.

I can honestly say, in that moment of time, I wondered if this was going to have a different ending. In the first story (his birth), he survived. *Would that be true again?* "God giveth, and God taketh away." Then I thought, well, we teamed up together like this before— we can certainly do it again. In that same moment, my heart recalled the miracle of the births of both Tyler and his older brother, Trevor.

Embrace the Spirit.
Its truth shall set you free.

DORENE STARK

chapter four

MIRACLE BIRTHS

First Fight for Life (Calamity One)

———— ⌇ ————

For you formed my inward parts; You covered me in my mother's womb. I will praise You, for I am fearfully and wonderfully made; Marvelous are Your works, and that my soul knows very well.

PSALM 139:13-14 NKJV

DORENE

Medically stated, neither one of our children should have survived. This is when we were taught, through the *Divine*, miracles still happen every day. With our first son, Trevor, my placenta stopped working during my eighth month, which meant the little guy was getting absolutely no nutrition for his entire ninth month. He was literally living off of his own baby fat! My body tried to warn me there were problems by giving me heavy contractions. At that moment, I went to the hospital, ready to deliver, but they sent me home saying everything was fine and I was overreacting. It was my first pregnancy, so I believed them and went home. I never really felt well after that, and my water started leaking ever so slightly but steadily. Again, since it was my first, I thought my bladder was just under pressure and becoming weak. Little did I know, the embryonic fluid was escaping me.

By the time Trevor was born, my fluid had been drained for an undetermined amount of time and my placenta was completely dead. At the end of forty weeks and exactly on his due date, it was only by the grace of God, this little four-pound bundle of a miracle was alive and healthy. Isn't it so often the case we see the miracle in hindsight? Perhaps if I had explained my "leaky" bladder situation to the doctor, they would have done some testing and possibly induced me or performed a C-section. Such a gift that God, in His infinite wisdom, knew this baby would be better off in the womb than in an incubator.

What were the consequences of the malnutrition for this little guy? It was discovered in the fourth grade he had a form of dyslexia called scotopic. When tested, his ability to read was at a college level yet his comprehension was at kindergarten level. This gave him some challenges during his school years, requiring much tutoring, especially at the college level, where he almost walked out and came home. Then, God did as God does and found Trevor an amazing counselor who identified the scotopic and provided a solution using colored transparencies. This allowed his brain to file information and recall it correctly. He went from Cs and Ds to As and Bs, getting an undergrad degree in Human Development and Family Studies and a master's degree in Organizational Psychology. That's how good God is, when we keep walking.

Tyler's Birth Story

It was a cold and blustery Monday morning with snow and blizzard conditions. Bruce was ready to walk out the door and head for work. We said our good-byes, but as he is closing the door behind him, I began to feel a bit strange. "Please wait. I think we may be having a situation here." He looked at me in disbelief. "Now? In the middle of a snowstorm on a Monday morning? You can't be serious!" Then he saw by the expression on my face that I was dead serious!

After checking off the list of all the "telltale" signs, we grabbed our bag, grabbed Trevor, called my mother, who planned to meet us at the hospital, and out the door we went, taking Trevor, quite unexpectedly, across the street to our kind neighbors, who were completely caught off guard. We had made arrangements for Trevor to go elsewhere but didn't have time to take him.

We didn't get too far when the contractions became quite intense. The traffic was heavy and crawling slowly. Here is where it begins to get complicated. . . . I have a

Rh-negative blood factor, and because Bruce is Rh-positive, this could cause a problem called Rh incompatibility. If Tyler's blood type was positive and his blood came into contact with mine during the pregancy or at delivery, my body would build antibodies against that positive Rh factor and mount an attack against Tyler's red blood cells. So typically, during the pregnancy and again after giving birth to each child, a RhoGAM shot is administered to alleviate any problems for the baby. *(RhoGAM: Rho(D) immune globulin is an injectable drug used to protect an Rh+ fetus from antibodies in an Rh- mother's blood and to prevent Rh allergy in the mother.)* I did receive this shot after the birth of Trevor. However, it was determined several months into my pregnancy with Tyler that the shot was ineffective, which only happens in about 1 percent of women. I was now classified as a high-risk pregnancy. Well, that was wonderful! So how was this going to be resolved? "Simple," they said, "we just give your child a blood transfusion upon his birth, and everything will be fine." Sounded great . . . until the alarm in my stomach went off again, and I was called to pay attention to that all-knowing voice of guidance. That voice firmly stated, *Absolutely not! Do not allow this to happen. I will show you a better way.* This was a fight I had to take on, so I began my quest. When I informed my OB-GYN and pediatric doctors we were not giving permission for the transfusion, they were less than pleased with us. This really complicated things for them.

They asked me why I was fighting against this so hard. "What is your fear and reasoning around this?" The problem with that question was that I didn't have any fear, nor did I have a reasonable answer for them. I just repeatedly had to say the truth. "I really don't know, except that I feel God is directing me this way, and I must be obedient to Him. There is a better way; we must simply find it." I had no medical knowledge to justify this, but I knew God did, and He is always faithful to our obedience.

Remember, this was 1983 and blood diseases in transfusions had not been discovered. AIDS had not yet been recognized, so medically speaking, there was no apparent reason not to move forward with the transfusion.

Faith begins where reason ends.

I want them to be encouraged and knit together by strong ties of love. I want them to have complete confidence that they understand God's mysterious plan, which is Christ himself.

COLOSSIANS 2:2 NLT

Long story short—many hours of phone calls, battling back and forth, resulted in our pediatrician doing some networking with other doctors, and they discovered there was another way! *Just like God said!* They would wash my blood, so it could then be given to Tyler. Finally, progress was made so we could move forward without a blood transfusion from the blood bank! Over several months, my blood was drawn, washed, cleaned, and was finally ready and waiting at Rose Hospital, which was about an hour's drive for us. We were about halfway there, and the contractions were strong and close together. In full labor at that point, I was overheating, so I rolled down the window to cool off as the snow blew in the window and my body was laid out in the front seat. I was holding on to the overhead bar while trying desperately to hold this baby inside, as he was struggling to come out. The gentleman in a large vehicle driving next to us happened to glance my way and shared a look on his face of shock and disbelief, one I will never forget! He probably won't either! As the time came to push, I knew I shouldn't, as I was trying with all my might to keep this baby inside. You see, we knew from my last doctor's appointment that the baby was breech, and we were all planning on a possible C-section delivery if he didn't turn on his own. Secretly, in my heart, I had been asking God all along if we could have a vaginal delivery. Well, you know the saying, "Be careful what you pray for." Here was how it unfolded.

The traffic was now in gridlock in both directions; we literally couldn't move! Suddenly, I felt something pop. I told Bruce, "We have got to get to a hospital, any hospital. Forget about getting to Rose Hospital. We are not even close, and this baby is coming out!" He could only hope this wasn't true and that this was not happening right now. However, it was happening! "Bruce, you must check and see what you can feel. Something has popped! I can't tell if it is the head or the feet!" Hesitating, he reached down between my legs and exclaims, "Oh, my God, Dorene, its feet are coming out!" I replied, "We must get to a hospital right away no matter what you have to do! Drive on the median, start honking your horn, anything, to get through this gridlock! Maybe we can attract the attention of a policeman to request a personal escort. You must hold your hand there and push its feet back. Don't let him come out!" (Quite impossible since he was driving a stick shift.) He calmly replied, "I can't push too hard; what if the legs break?" In the meantime, I was thinking, "Oh, dear God, how long can this child stay in the birth canal and not suffocate? What are we to do?" The only thing I *knew* to do was to give the situation to God and just try to listen for the guiding voice to come through. That quiet whisper in the midst of my storm.

Breathe.

This was my *first* experience of what it means to give my child back to God. (Oh, how He prepared us for the years ahead.)

God, I have no control over this situation. It is life-threatening to this child, and my only hope is in understanding this child truly belongs to you, to do with as you please.

Whatever your will is right here, right now, what-ever the outcome is, it will be perfect. You will either be giving us a beautiful child, or we will be giving you a beautiful angel. I am accepting whatever choice you make for this baby's life.

It is usually in our most desperate times that we finally surrender and let God take charge. It was the same for me. It was the moment I put my desires aside and let the will of God prevail in my heart that I was able to hear Him whisper, *Do not go to Rose Hospital. Turn around and go to Porter.* I conveyed this message to Bruce, which confirmed the message he had already been given. He immediately crossed the median and made a U-turn. Off we went to the nearest hospital, which was still a good distance away, and traffic was still backed up. As you can imagine, people were angry and honking, flipping us off and yelling out their windows at us. For us, it was all for the life of our child!

Finally, upon our arrival, Bruce came close to hitting two doctors as he pulled up into the emergency drive-way. He jumped out of the car and rattled off about his wife giving birth. Their response was, "We are really sorry, but we don't deliver babies here. We don't treat children under twelve years old. You will need to drive to Swedish Hospital." Bruce responded abruptly, "Well, you are today because this child is almost here, feet first! His legs are hanging out, and someone needs to help us!"

With that, they were convinced and rushed out with a stretcher.

Once in the emergency room, the doctor calmly said, "Well, I am not sure how this is going to go, Dorene. I have never delivered a breech baby before." I replied in desperation, "Hey, that makes two of us, because I haven't either! Let's do this!" (Sometimes a birthing mother loses her kindness.)

Little Feet

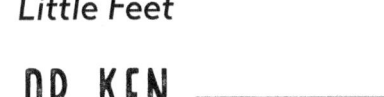

DR. KEN

It was December 5, 1983, and I had been working as a part-time emergency physician at Porter Hospital in Denver for about a year as I completed my additional training in Medical Toxicology. In my last year of Emergency Medicine training at Denver General Hospital, I did an elective rotation for a month on the Labor Deck, primarily because the chief resident was a friend and she promised I would deliver many babies myself, which I certainly did. But *never* a breech baby—those go to C-section and are not delivered on the Labor Deck. But I learned to remain calm during the crisis moments of a difficult birth, how to perform an episiotomy, where an incision is made to enlarge the birth canal, and how to get all the resuscitation equipment ready for a newborn that might be born very ill.

It was early in the morning. I had just begun my first solo shift in the ER, when a nurse informed me there was a car in the ambulance bay with a woman in labor. When I walked to the car and looked down at the patient in the passenger seat, I could see two tiny little feet dangling down. I immediately knew the baby, the mother, and myself were all in very serious trouble.

Porter Hospital did not have a Labor Deck at that time, so there were no obstetric doctors or nurses in the hospital. I asked the nurse to try to find some OB doc to come in emergently, and we got the patient onto an exam table that had gyn stirrups. Still only two little feet showing, I desperately searched my brain data banks to try to remember from my OB textbook the techniques on how to deliver what is called "a footling breach."

With one push—*finally allowed*—his little body was now almost fully exposed. Everything was out now except for his head. It was stuck at the chin! I had no idea what to do now and expressed my concern about how long this baby had been in the birth canal. "The only way I have a chance to save him is to go in with both hands and pull him out. This will be very painful since you have not been given any drugs," I explained to Dorene.

Gentle pressure and rotation with pushing from the mother got the legs, chest, and arms delivered, but the head was not going to come, as the baby's chin was firmly stuck. An episiotomy was done to enlarge the birth canal, but now the baby's little body was turning a darker blue. The situation was looking critical. I remember a feeling of absolute helplessness, that I just couldn't do this myself. And then, although I had only a very weak faith at the time, my terrified mind asked God to help me get this baby out.

With renewed effort, knowing this baby was not going to live or be normal unless his head came out right now, I had to slightly push the baby back up into the birth canal, rotate the body, and insert my fingers into the miniscule space between chin and bone. Now, it was time to push.

"Okay then," said Dorene. While looking at me, between heavy breaths, she said, "Let's do it!" At that point, she let out a cry of pain that Bruce could hear from the waiting room outside the door.

With an audible whoosh, the head was delivered, the blue baby handed off to the waiting nurses to get him warmed up, and the placenta delivered. APGAR scores were good, and the crisis seemed to be over.

DORENE

Another boy! How perfect! The doctors had suspected all along we were to have a girl, but being the tom-girl I was growing up with brothers, I was delighted and overjoyed to have two boys. I was never very good at playing house and Barbie dolls. Get me out for some flag football, the soccer field, basketball court, or on the back of a horse and look out! My brothers had coached me well. So, this was very comfortable for me. I understand the ways of brotherly bonding.

It was a moment we needed to acknowledge that both of our children truly belonged to God, and we were only their keepers until such a time that God called them home. As I gazed upon these beautiful infants, each miracle of life that was given us, I said, "Lord, we will do our best to raise him to be pleasing to you, as we are so honored to have the privilege of your child in our charge." This phrase came back to me years later.

For now, though, let's re-engage here. We have another issue—*the blood*! Following our brief "hello" moment, Tyler was whisked away, wrapped in a towel, and laid on a cold utensil tray. No sweet little infant beds or tiny blankets here since they were not equipped for babies. My washed and cleaned blood was still sitting in a distant hospital, unattainable, so the transfusion my pediatrician had ordered upon birth was not going to happen. As we explained to the ER doctor about Tyler's need for a transfusion, he immediately wanted to get him transferred to Swedish Hospital, where they are equipped with an intensive care unit for infants. Even though this would go against everything my doctor had planned for, I found that sweet peace, knowing God had changed our course, for His will to be done.

It "just so happened" a fire truck had just delivered a heart patient to the hospital, and the fireman overheard all the commotion about this child needing to get to Swedish Hospital. They kindly volunteered to bring Tyler to the hospital for us. He was sure to get through the snow and traffic with sirens and horns, no problem! Just what we needed at just the right time! A coincidence?

Meanwhile, my poor mother had finally made her way to Rose Hospital, enduring a tense and treacherous drive, only to find we had not arrived. Talk about panic! I was finally able to have the ER nurse contact the hospital and let Mom know we would be moving from Porter Hospital to Swedish Hospital, and she could meet us there (no cell phones at this time). They gave her no additional information, so of course, she had no idea what had happened and whether everything was all right or not. Finally, she arrived, and our eyes locked. No words, just tears. Bruce had to stay with me while I received stitches, and baby Tyler was off for a ride in the firetruck without us. I couldn't wait to hold him!

DR. KEN

As the doctor in this situation, I was relieved after baby and family were safely sent to another hospital that had a neonatal intensive care unit. Needing a few moments of reflection, I proceeded to the doctor's lounge off the ER and mentally collapsed. Looking back, over a total of twenty years as an emergency physician, I had never had such a scary moment. I just couldn't move or think for a few minutes. But my ER shift had just started, and now, I had many other patients to see, and I had to get them cared for.

DORENE

Now at the NICU, as God would have it, all of the new-born tests came out very well, with the exception of the blood factor. However, at this point, they were not critical yet, so we had some breathing room, or so we thought. The next day, his levels began to fluctuate. At this point, the doctors explained Tyler's body contained two different types of blood that were not compatible. This is where the RhoGAM shot did not work for me. One blood type would try to combat the other in a continuous fight between the two until one wins, or his body fails him and gives up. Feeling certain now that God did not want the transfusion (which was my doctor's request), we searched for the right answer.

My pediatrician consulted with a doctor at Children's Hospital who had done some research in this area. His advice was to wait it out and see what Tyler's body would do on its own. Five weeks later at his follow-up appointment, we were informed of his low blood counts. Another test was necessary in one week. A week later, his blood counts continued to drop, and the doctors urgently requested the transfusion. We declined for the third time. We consulted again with the previous doctor. If we could help Tyler's own blood take over the foreign blood, rather than my washed blood, it would be far more beneficial. His recommendation was to give Tyler large doses of folic acid for one week and to monitor him closely. He said the first *three* days would be critical (such biblical significance).

We followed these instructions and kept watch over him day and night as he continued to lose weight, turn yellow with jaundice, and just seemed to lay so still, so helpless. The second day, we called upon our family friend and priest, Monsignor Heister, to come and anoint him with sacred oils and pray over him. The third day came, and he was still not looking any better. We decided at that point, we needed a timeline. We agreed on noon. I am not exaggerating this. By noon, he looked like a completely different child. His eyes were opened wide, much brighter than before, and his color was slowly returning to normal. The doctor, of course, wanted confirmation. Instructions were two more days of folic acid and then more tests.

A trip back to the doctor's office to run a few tests, in fact, confirmed that Tyler's own blood has won the fight and he is now on his way to perfect health. Praise God! We can refer to this as his second fight for life. (*Calamity Two*) Our hearts were so filled with joy and gratitude. Now, we knew the reason why God did not allow us to get to Rose Hospital that day. He did not want this child transfused at all, knowing that a full healing was already in His plan. We had trusted Him completely, with orchestrating everything, allowing Him to fulfill His will. A beautiful manifestation of His love and faithfulness.

Here's the kicker to end that story.

It was about two years later that we saw an interesting story on the evening news. It was about a little boy who was born just weeks after Tyler. The child had come down with a terrible illness that, within those two years, would sadly consume the life of this precious child. It was the first known case of AIDS being transmitted by a blood transfusion. This was the same blood bank the doctor recommended we use. It really took me off guard when I put the dates together and realized that this could have easily been Tyler! How beautiful and faithful is our God when we surrender and allow Him to be in complete control!

Let's define "surrender." Dictionary.com defines it as "to give oneself up, as into the power of another; submit or yield." This is clearly different than becoming a "victim"—"a person who is deceived or cheated, as by their own emotions or ignorance, a person who suffers from a destructive action." It is our choice to decide which path to follow: beat down and broken, or surrendering control and standing as a warrior when needed. So, standing in my truth—against the advice of medical doctors—for a transfusion, with no explanation to back up my conviction other than God, He brought another sweet gift of pure love.

This was where God really laid the groundwork in me, teaching me and preparing me, for the events that were to come during Tyler's deployment with the Air Force.

• • •

We were so grateful for the events that took place on that snowy Monday morning that it only seemed fitting to return to Porter Hospital to thank the staff for the work they had done, especially the doctors on duty that day. After things had settled down, I made a trip to the hospital to seek them out, only to be disappointed. No one seemed to be able to track down the doctors or their whereabouts! Emergency room rotations were not dictated by the hospitals, so my request became quite challenging for them. Not knowing the ins and outs of their rotations, the staff were unable to assist me any further. I left feeling a little bit empty that the doctor who saved the life of our child would not know the gratitude we felt in our hearts. The best I could do (which I did) was to leave a card for him in hopes that someday, it would find him. It was always a desire of my heart to make that connection, but over time, it seemed less and less probable, so I tucked the desire away deep in my heart, hoping God would bless that doctor in a special way.

Over time, we might often forget the prayers and desires of our hearts, but God never forgets. It would be thirty-four years later that He would show up again with a "divine design" to retrieve that desire I had casually tucked away.

Upon receiving a promotion in my school position, a class I had to attend would allow me to meet a colleague that would later become a very dear friend. Ten years after our first meeting and after numerous evenings together, we set up a dinner engagement on this particular Sunday evening. This in itself was unusual, because as many times as we had met for dinner over the years, we had never met up on a Sunday, and this date was planned a month in advance. Why does this matter? Well, it just so happened that only days prior to meeting our friends, Karen and Ed, they became grandparents.

Over dinner, they were explaining that their daughter's baby was coming out breech! During labor, she needed to be taken for a C-section. As soon we heard the word "breech," we were prompted to share our story about Tyler's breech birth. During the story, our friends kept looking at each other with questioning looks and chuckles. The curiosity was killing us, so we begged them to explain their nonverbal communication, but they refused until we had finished our story. Then they shared theirs.

"Would you believe that we heard the very same story this morning after church?"

"*What?*" we replied. "How could that possibly be?" It was such a unique story. Certainly, there couldn't be another one like it, could there?

"It's true," they replied. "A doctor friend of ours at church responded with this very same story when we spoke to him about our daughter's breech birth experience."

Karen decided we should text the doctor to verify some of the details. We all agreed. She sent him a list of questions regarding the date, year, time, and location of the event. His response was "yes" to all of the questions and then included a question of his own. "Why are you asking me all of these questions?" Karen's reply was simply, "I believe we are sitting with the parents of the child you were speaking about this morning!" Well, you can imagine his surprise at that moment. Frankly, we were all in disbelief as more details unfolded.

Without hesitation, we all agreed to meet the following Sunday to share our experiences. Wouldn't it be beautiful to complete the story for all of us? In the thirty-four years that had passed by in our lives, the opportunity to come together and share these different experiences had not been presented to us. Not only that, but we would finally be able to say "thank you," in person! What are the odds? Rejoicing in this unimaginable possibility, we wondered how we could ever appropriately express our gratitude to Dr. Ken Kulig.

We began the search for the perfect gift. At Tyler's infant baptism, his father, Bruce, was given a lapel pin (gifted by Tyler's godfather) that symbolizes the Right to Life group, a pair of tiny footprints. We all have one now to commemorate the "feet-first" birth. We were also given a plaque with the famous "Footprints" poem on it. This quickly became our family's token of a special memory in our lives. We decided it would be most fitting for the doctor to have a pin as well. It took some searching, but we were successful. We also wanted to include him in the "Footprints" poem and came across a lovely sandstone-etched plaque. It was perfect! We purchased two of them, so the doctor and his patient could share the same memento. Since the doctor knew nothing about

Tyler and his life, we thought it would be helpful for him to have a few photos. After sharing these pictures with the doctor, it prompted him to share with us his own faith experience.

DR. KEN

After moments of exchanging stories, I found myself reflecting upon the pictures presented to me by Tyler's parents. I was quickly taken back to the moment when I held a feet-first blue baby in my hands, and now I was staring at these pictures of this young man thirty-four years later. It is absolutely stunning how God interweaves life's connections; to see how, from something that was such a miracle many years ago, God has continued to bless and protect Tyler's journey leaves me in awe. But, as the TV commercial says, "Wait, there's more!"

While going through the pictures and learning of Tyler's life, I thought of my own two sons and the faith experience that changed my life: Columbine. That is when the parents told me their son, Little Feet from thirty-four years ago, was a student at Columbine on that day and, in fact, was chased up a stairwell while avoiding active bullets. At that point during our gathering, I lost it. I had to pause and just go blank, like I did in the doctor's lounge after Little Feet was born. It was that moment when I realized Little Feet had saved my life, not the other way around.

Our breakfast meeting.
(L to R) Karen and Ed Loar, Rose and Dr. Ken Kulig,
Dorene and Bruce Stark

On April 20, 1999, after the shooting at Columbine High School was revealed for the horror it was, I left my office to go home to be with my kids. On the way, I saw a sign for a blood drive and so I donated blood. Then, as I drove toward home, I noticed that the sky was dark and evil-appearing like I had never seen it before. There was a battle going on, right there in Littleton, between evil and good, Satan and God.

After I got the kids to bed, I picked up a Bible I had purchased only a few months before and started reading Matthew. At that time, my faith was lukewarm at best, where I believed there was a God, but believing Jesus was God was difficult. But on that night, Jesus spoke to me personally and said, "Are you finally ready to follow me?" I knew I had a choice; I had free will and I could have easily said, "Sorry, not yet." But instead, I said to the Lord without reservation, "Yes, Lord. I'm ready. I will follow you forever."

And so I did. He taught me how to talk to patients about God. He taught me how to give Bibles to patients, to give hope to those who had none. He taught me how my pride had kept us apart, and that was okay, it just was. And so many other things in my life, including Little Feet's story, finally made sense.

REFLECTION

The purpose of sharing this story with you is to share a real-life event that once again shows the power of *faith*, *trust*, and *obedience*. *Faith* enough to know *God can*. *Trust* enough to know *God will*, and the *obedience* to listen to His gentle whisper.

Where was the faith?

Knowing God was in control yet again and staying out of God's way. God did not want us to make it to Rose Hospital for the blood transfusion, so He sent us in a different direction. Do you think the snowstorm and timing of rush-hour traffic was a coincidence?

Where was the trust?

In my limited mind, my original vision was getting him blood no matter what. I thought that was God's plan. If you are a mother reading this, you know we will stop at nothing for the life of our child. We could have pulled over at the next gas station and called the police for an escort. Instead, trust prevailed when we heard the gentle whisper, the one that said, "Go back, go back to the hospital you have already passed and put him in my care." Bruce and I agreed.

Where was the obedience?

We made the U-turn. The panic subsided and we "let go." What if we had not listened? What if we had not stepped out of God's way? We always have a choice. Again, try to recall your own experiences to bring an awareness to your own life struggles and situations. Try to recognize where God is working in your life.

• • •

It is also important to see how faith and trust are very different, yet they must work together.

Trust puts faith into action.
Obedience brings the results.

chapter five

THE SPIN

What, then, shall we say in response to these things?
If God is for us, who can be against us?

ROMANS 8:31

Mask (Tyler) & MeSo (Ken) waiting for take-off in an F-15 fighter jet at the NATO airbase in Aviano, Italy, Monday, March 21, 2011. (AP Photo/Luca Bruno)

TYLER

As we flew away from Libya to get our strike package together, MeSo noticed our right external tank was not

Photo by: Staff Sgt. Michael Battles

Jet in flight

feeding out its fuel. If we couldn't fix this, it meant we had to go home. We ran the checklist and couldn't get it to feed gas. Fortunately, due to his experience, MeSo had a trick. We had been flying above thirty-thousand feet all night to avoid the anti-aircraft threats, and there was a chance some water had simply frozen in the line connecting the tank to the jet. So, while clear of any threats, we dropped down to ten-thousand feet to melt the ice, and sure enough, the tank started feeding, albeit pretty slowly, but we were back in the fight.

The tasking was 2xGBU-38s, which are each 500 lb. GPS-guided weapons. Now that we were good, MeSo requested each aircraft drop one bomb in order for me to get a "drop" on my first combat sortie. They agreed and passed the coordinates for the target, an anti-aircraft site, which I verified were input correctly into the weapon and the fuse appropriately set. We have the capability of using our radar to create a map, and so we started our mapping leg to verify the coordinates while Weasel flight of two F16CMs pushed in front of us. There were surface to air missiles in the area, and the Weasels were going to shoot pre-emptive HARM missiles that lock on to any SAM radar that was on to hopefully destroy it before they had a chance to shoot at us.

Compared to the wars in Afghanistan, this was a pretty full up first mission with other aircraft and missiles coming off jets. This was something that didn't happen in Afghanistan, and I was lucky enough to be a part of it. As we approached the release point, MeSo queried, "Confirm my bomb," which is crew coordination indicating everything is accurate in the weapon and it's ready for release. I gave him the response, "Cleared to release," and he hit the pickle button and released the weapon.

This was where things started to diverge from what we planned. Based on the high fuel weight (since we had just gotten a top-up), the remaining seven bombs, and flying at thirty-two thousand feet, the jet did not have the performance we were used to. We knew this, and MeSo intentionally made an easy turn to the right to go the opposite direction we had come from, but 90 degrees, or halfway, through the turn the jet started to buffet (rumble), as we were asking too much of it. The buffet increased, and the nose began to fall to 30 degrees, nose low. Not sure if he was responding to a threat I hadn't seen yet, or if he was trying to get airspeed back, I asked MeSo, "Uh, what are we doing?" His response was one you don't want to hear over combat territory, "The jet departed." What he meant was the jet was no longer responding to his inputs! Thankfully, the jet is very resilient, and you can recover easily. Step one is to release the controls, let the aircraft start flying again and gain some airspeed, all of which we were already doing. We were nose low for only three to four seconds when MeSo slowly started to bring the nose back to the horizon to level our flight. As the nose got closer to the horizon, the jet started to enter a spin to the left. Flying at a higher altitude, fully loaded with bombs, with full fuel, in thinner air, one side higher than the other is not a typical situation!

The F-15 Strike Eagle has a robust flight control system, with the intelligence to know it's in a spin, along with the ability to correct and overcome numerous flying situations. Unfortunately, in this situation, that was not happening. As the spin rapidly increased in speed, it threw us violently forward in our seats with a very uncomfortable eyes-popping-out feeling. It took both of us a second or two for our vision to adjust as the lights and voice cautions in the jet started to go off, "Over-G, Over-G...Yaw Rate, Yaw Rate."

Before I could verify that the throttles and stick matched the screen, I had to remove several items that had been thrown forward on the screens due to the centripetal force. As I went to verify the stick and throttles were in the right position, I realized I had made an error several hours ago in my haste to get strapped in. Normally, the stick is between your legs, and when it is full left stick, which it was, it should be touching your inner thigh. It was underneath my leg, below and behind my knee by several inches. In fact, I was barely touching the seat. The error I had made three hours earlier was not tightening my lap belt tight enough. Although this was intentional, as I wanted free movement to check behind us at our six o'clock, it was a grave decision now.

I was thrown forward and somewhat floating as we were fully established in a spin over Libya. Now I knew our control inputs were correct, I started keeping both of us aware of our altitude. The first one I called out was twenty-six thousand feet. *We have already lost seven thousand feet in only a matter of seconds!* MeSo made a radio call to #1, *"Two's in a spin . . ."* Our flight lead thought something went wrong on the target attack, assuming we did not release our bomb and were spinning around to attempt it again and acknowledged with a "1." He did not realize we were in a flat spin, and our situation was grave.

Another two thousand-foot drop! Now, at twenty-four thousand feet, we had plenty of time to recover the jet, but altitude was beginning to tick by, and the spin had not started to slow. I knew underneath us was hostile territory and a place I had no plans on visiting, but time was running out as we approached our out of control bail out altitude of six thousand feet. As the aircraft settled into the spin, I finally sank back into my seat, but I was still being forced forward as if a four-hundred-pound man was pulling me out of my seat. I knew if this continued and we got to six thousand feet, we would have to eject, and I was not in a good body position to do so, as I knew my knees would not clear the display. They would be torn to shreds.

I tried grabbing the fabric of the seat and sliding myself back, but the force was too difficult to overcome. The only way I could get myself to the back of my seat was to push off the displays with both hands. If I had my hands extended when we ejected, they would probably clear the displays, but as soon as I hit the windstream, they would most likely both be dislocated and broken in a flailing injury. That one mistake of not strapping in tight enough before we even started the jet could now have catastrophic effects!

As I called out "fifteen thousand feet," the nose of the jet started to slow, and I had a quick moment of celebration as I thought we are pulling the jet out of the spin. I had a hopeful feeling that we still had time to recover the jet from the spin, yet every second that passed we lost more altitude, bringing us closer to our minimum ejection altitude of six thousand feet. No sooner had the nose started to slow indicating we might be recovering from the spin, it quickly accelerated and we were once again established in a spin.

I had this strong sinking feeling, and I was not alone. MeSo called out *"Two's in a spin; mayday, mayday, mayday!"* as we passed through twelve thousand feet. His call left nothing up to interpretation and #1 quickly got on the radio and started backing us up with altitudes, "Two, you're at twelve thousand." As the last few thousand feet disappeared above us, I knew where we were headed—to an ejection. In that moment of terror, I could have called for the ejection earlier to allow us more time under canopy, which could have helped with orientating ourselves for the evading that would soon follow, but my brain was fixated on waiting until we hit six thousand feet to give the call.

When #1 called "Two, you're at nine thousand," MeSo thought he heard "five thousand" and gave the command of execution, "Bailout, bailout, bailout!" But since he thought we were below our minimum ejection altitude he said those three words and pulled the handles as soon as the last bailout was out of his mouth.

At this point, we had no indicators or warnings from our jet of our demise. The result would be a fighter jet spinning out of control, because it was severely out of balance. Once the plane began to spin and descend, there was no getting it back. Our flight put this amazing jet to a test it had not been previously asked to perform. Unfortunately, we ran out of emergency options, and the jet was not able to recover.

We followed our emergency procedures for an "out of control" aircraft that was in a spin, but the imbalance proved more than the aircraft could overcome, and we were forced to eject.

If you have seen the movie *Top Gun*, you would have a fairly accurate viewing of what was going on inside of our cockpit. If you recall in the movie, Goose (the backseat officer) did not survive the ejection. Fortunately for me, in this case, he survived!

Time seemed to slow down as I reached for the handles and got a good grip on only one. I leaned back as much as I could to get in a good body position. Then I felt the canopy jettison and the cool night air rush over me. Before I could even process that, I felt a kick in the butt as the rocket ignited and began shooting me upward away from the jet. I remember hitting the windstream and seeing the nose of the jet fade away from me in the red light of the rocket motor. The safety of that cockpit, the one that was meant to take me home and away from enemy territory was disappearing below me . . . then WHAM!

The ejection wasn't pleasant, but the opening shock of the parachute canopy inflating straight up hurt. It jolted me back to reality. The force of it, made me look at my feet, where I saw MeSo's canopy about ten feet below me. Part of me wanted to kick his canopy, as he had promised me before we stepped to the jet that "everything was going to be fine." *This was anything but "fine"!* The urge quickly passed, and I was just glad he made it safely out of the aircraft. Then, I took a quick inventory of my own body parts . . . YES! My limbs were all intact and accounted for! (It is not uncommon to lose limbs or die when ejecting, as the body hits the airwall at approximately five hundred miles an hour.) One deep breath gave me a moment to experience relief flooding over my entire body. This was *Top Gun* in reality! (*Calamity Three*) Now to immediately refocus.

In the military, there is a checklist for everything; one of which is the post-ejection checklist. I was familiar with it and had gone through it many times in parachute training. Obviously, that was parasailing, and this was jumping out of an aircraft. Which I had never done before! It's pretty straight forward: canopy, visor, mask, seat kit, 4-lines, steer, prepare to land. Of course, my first thought was, "You have to be *&%#ing me!" This was my first mission. I should still be in the safe comfort of the jet, not floating in a canopy over *hostile territory! This is not how this was supposed to happen! It's still not over!*

Canopy . . . Visor . . . Mask . . . Seat Kit . . . 4-lines . . . Steer . . . Prepare to Land . . .

As I attempted to check the canopy, I realized I couldn't because the risers (ropes) were twisted and forcing me to look down. No problem; I remembered the training—reach above your head and pull apart the risers while bicycle kicking in the air and you will untwist. The first part was easy enough. The raft, which was attached to the seat kit, had deployed appropriately, but due to the spinning momentum of the plane, it had wrapped itself around my legs. I was tied up! As I worked the raft line free of my legs, I began to bicycle kick, and in ten to fifteen seconds, I had fixed the twisted line.

As I was fixing the line, I saw where the jet had impacted on the ground. It was now just a large fireball. As I rotated around a second time, I could see a missile that initially looked like it was headed toward me. I remember the sick feeling! I wasn't able to see where it was shot from, just the smoke trail. After all that had happened, I couldn't believe they were now shooting missiles at me under canopy. By the time I rotated around again, it was clear the missile was not aiming at me. *Whew!*

Looking back, of course, they were not shooting a missile at me. Most are either heat-seekers (a person doesn't have enough heat for the missile to guide on) or they go where you point them like an RPG. Both would be a poor choice to hit someone in a canopy at several thousand feet. I found out later that it was a missile on our jet that eventually cooked off due to the hot fire when the jet crashed.

Seeing the missile made me realize how vulnerable I was just sitting in my parachute floating down. I began to fear that someone on the ground might see me and start shooting whatever they could at me.

Finally, I was able to look at my chute and make sure it was fully inflated with no line tangles and in good condition. Our parachutes are made of thirteen long panels, stitched together to make a circle. I saw from looking at the top of the canopy, about a quarter of the way down on one of the panels was a massive hole! The hole spanned all the way to the bottom. *Man! Nothing seems to be going my way today!* Knowing there was nothing at this point I could do about it, I continued on with the checklist.

Visor: We didn't have one because we were wearing NVGs, which you were supposed to remove if you had time before ejection, so they didn't crush your "nether" region on ejection, or if by chance they stayed on through ejection, so they didn't come off into your eyes when you hit the wind stream and break your eye sockets. Neither one of us removed ours, but I didn't have them now. Thankfully, we sustained no damage from them.

Mask: You are supposed to unclamp the bayonets on each side that holds it onto the helmet and pull, with fourteen pounds of pressure, to remove the air hose that feeds into the helmet. I pulled the bayonets but didn't pull hard enough to remove the mask completely, so it ended up dangling low, but was no factor.

Seat Kit: If it is oscillating, you can unclip one side. Mine was fine so I left both attached.

LPU (Life preserver unit—inflatables): At night, you are supposed to inflate these, as you can't see if you are going to land in water. But we both knew that we were over desert, and so neither one of us pulled the red tabs to inflate them. Good thing, as it is like a horse collar around your neck and makes visibility below you that much more difficult.

4-lines: These are two red handles, which, when pulled, sever four lines from the canopy, giving you more ability to steer and some forward travel for a softer landing. I had to pause on this one as I reached deep into my memory, in an attempt to recall the training rule of thumb for how large a hole you can have and still cut the 4-lines. I couldn't remember, but I felt like since it was a massive hole, it would not be good to pull the handles. This ended up being a moot point because as I was thinking about it,

I started to look at the loops that should be there, only to discover the left one was sheared off. I couldn't have pulled it even if I wanted to!

Steer: Without the 4-lines pulled, you have to pull with all your weight on a riser in order to turn the parachute away from the crash. I couldn't get the parachute to turn, so I surrendered to the direction I was going. Thankfully, I was drifting away from the crash.

Prepare to Land: At this moment, feeling somewhat dejected and that truly nothing was going my way, I had a moment of peacefulness wash over me. It was a cool night, with only a few clouds in the sky and a beautiful full moon that captured my attention as it lit up the dark night. A moment I will never forget. It was short-lived, however, as I started to make out features of the rapidly approaching ground. I knew if I had any chance of evading, I needed to survey the surrounding area for roads, houses, cars, or any activity that might give me the best initial direction on a large scale. It was important in this brief moment to build a mental map from the birds-eye view I would lose upon hitting the ground.

As the ground started to get closer, I prepared to land by sticking my legs together, bending my knees, keeping my eyes on the horizon, and attempting the best PLF (parachute landing fall) of my life. I found out later that, based on the hole in my parachute, I was descending at a rate of fifty percent faster than I should have been. My hands were on the fittings to release the parachute as soon as I was safely down. As the ground approached, my heart started to race. There was no wind! I had no forward movement! I was coming down like a sack of potatoes!

What I trained for, but thought would never happen.

BULLETS WERE RICOCHETING OFF OF THE LOCKERS, AND DUST FROM THE CEILING TILES WAS FALLING ALL AROUND ME. IT FELT LIKE A WAR ZONE. I HAD NOWHERE TO HIDE, AND I WAS ALONE.

chapter 6

THE MASSACRE

Tyler Stark hit the desert floor in what he believed was a perfect position. "I thought I did a pretty good job, but halfway through I hear this 'pop' and I fall on my butt." He'd torn tendons in both his left knee and his left ankle. He looked around for shelter. There was nothing but a few chest-high thornbushes and some small rocks. He was in the middle of the desert; there was no place to hide. I need to get away from this area, he thought. He collected the gear he wanted, stuffed the rest in a thornbush, and began to move. "The moment of serenity had gone away," he recalled. It was his first combat mission, but he'd felt the way he now felt once before: during Columbine."[2]

— MICHAEL LEWIS, journalist
Vanity Fair, 10 Issues 2012

---

[2] Michael Lewis, "Obama's Way," *Vanity Fair*, September 11, 2012. *www.vanityfair.com/news/2012/10/michael-lewis-profile-barack-obama*.

Columbine – Setting the Stage

TYLER

Feeling unsettled, I tried to call my mom who worked at an elementary school in the same school district. Someone helping in the office put me on hold. I had no way of knowing how chaotic her school was at this time, as they were under lockdown and parents were frantic. Well, I was frantic too, and I felt like those moments on hold were an eternity. Kids were shooting at us! I dropped the phone and started running.

The Monday prior to this event seemed normal, with no signs of anything that might take place the next day, except for an altercation my brother Trevor had with Eric Harris.

TREVOR

It was passing period, so many students were in the hallway moving from class to class. I happened to see a friend of mine at his locker, so while I was walking by him, we exchanged a few friendly words. At this moment, I was more focused on my friend, than where I was walking and just so happened to bump sideways into Eric Harris, causing our backpacks to slide off our shoulders. He made it quite clear he was angry about the incident. I reminded him it was an accident, and he didn't own the hallway.

His reply to my boldness was a chuckle, followed by a sarcastic, "Have a nice day tomorrow!" Though I thought his remark was a bit odd, I let it roll off my back. Since he was part of the "Trench Coats," a comment with some sarcasm would not be unusual. Little did I know what he was referencing!

The following day, April 20, 1999, I was going to use my study hall and lunchtime to go home and prepare for a test I had that afternoon. We had just had our Senior Prom the week before, and my Prom date (who did not attend Columbine) had left her purse at school. So, before I left, I headed to the office to pick it up for her. Upon arriving at the office, the place seemed rather busy, and there was already a line. I didn't want to waste what little time I had, so I proceeded out the door toward the parking lot. While making my way to my car, I saw both Eric and Dylan getting out of their car, wearing their customary trench coats, but nothing that seemed unusual to me.

TYLER

Tuesday morning was completely normal for me. Then something changed....

I *always* went to the library during my study hall hour. However, oddly enough, some friends (Nathan and Brad) who I had not seen in quite some time convinced me to sit with them during their lunch break. *How could I have known their persuasion would save my life?*

Another fellow student, Michael, sat down to join us for lunch. Nathan began giving him a hard time, to the point Michael felt he wasn't welcome. He abruptly left our table and went outside.

Eric Harris and Dylan Klebold's plan was supposed to start at 11:10 that morning. Without anyone taking notice, they had placed propane bombs in bags next to the support beam pillars inside the cafeteria. The intent of the bombs was to collapse the library, which was directly above the cafeteria. This potentially could have killed approximately four hundred students, including myself. To this day, I still ponder how the bombs were brought in, yet were not noticed by anyone?

When the bombs did not go off at 11:10, they took matters into their own hands and entered the school at 11:17, targeting mainly the jocks (identified by the white baseball caps from various colleges they wore) and anyone else they could find to shoot. The first indication something was wrong was when Mr. Sanders came into the cafeteria yelling for everyone to "get down." No one knew what was going on. It felt like a drill. The table I was sitting at was close to the window, so I crawled the two or three feet over to the window to look outside, and I saw Michael about fifteen feet away—the student sitting with us just a few minutes before. He picked himself up off the ground and then began to walk but was limping. I noticed his pant leg was shredded. I could clearly see his leg was bleeding. My first thought was he must have fallen and scuffed up his leg. What else could have happened? In reality, he had been shot! He had gone outside after leaving our table and was one of the first students to be shot outside by Dylan.

At this point, I saw Dylan walk down the cement stairs outside the cafeteria. I recognized him as a student at Columbine, but I was not friends with him. He was dressed in a black trench coat, black pants, and some type of military looking boots. He was holding something in his left hand. It appeared to be a semiautomatic pistol with a long magazine. Hanging on his right side was a type of shotgun with a sling on it. In his right hand, he was holding what looked like a sand weight. He lit it and threw it in the parking lot next to a Jeep. I saw a puff of white smoke, but no damage appeared to the cars, so I thought it was just a stunt. I was still trying to assess what was going on. I assumed it was just a smoke bomb to pull a senior prank of some kind. However, at the same time, it felt a little more serious. At that point, he started approaching the side entrance to the cafeteria. Mr. Sanders told everyone to "run!"

From there, it was fight or flight, and I definitely chose the "flight" option. As the panic increased, hundreds and hundreds of kids began running up the stairs, jumping over backpacks, chairs, and tables, as well as each other. It was just a blur, trying to make my way up the stairs. About halfway through the cafeteria, Dylan began shooting into the crowd. I didn't grow up with guns, so I was unfamiliar with what being shot at from afar sounded like. It sounded just like firecrackers, but I knew they were bullets. There wasn't time to process what was happening around me. A sense of fear was driving me away from the cafeteria and from Dylan. As everyone started running up the stairs, it felt like the other students were feeling the same thing. As my friend Brad and I ran up the stairs, we lost track of Nathan in the chaos.

At the top of the stairs were the science halls, and the teachers were frantically trying to usher students into the rooms for safety. In that moment, I was still very much in the "flight" response. There was still plenty of hallway for me to run, so I continued down the main hall toward the exit. I wasn't sure what made me keep running to the exit and away from my science teacher, who was directing students into the science hall. I felt my best option was to escape from the building instead of hiding inside. I knew I needed to get out of the situation, though I hadn't processed what the situation actually was. Brad decided to peel off toward the science room. As a result, he ended up being locked in there with a group of students for several hours. During this time, they were continually harassed by Eric and Dylan, who were shooting bullets through the door, which had been barricaded to keep them out! In addition, they threw pipe bombs at the base of the door, trying to flush out the students or gain access before the SWAT team eventually came to their rescue.

As I was running down the main hall, I saw one hundred to two hundred students at the exit. It was clear there was a logjam of students trying to get out. I knew

I couldn't just stand there waiting to get out if Dylan was walking up the stairs to begin shooting into the crowd. So, I came up with what I thought was a good idea. I would go down the middle hallway that connected to the other main hallway and the other main exit. I thought this was brilliant, thinking the other students would clue in and follow me. So, I made the turn, getting about fifteen to twenty feet down the connecting hallway. I turned around and realized no one had followed me. I was alone in the connecting hallway and feeling somewhat afraid to be away from the group, but I was committed at this point.

As I proceeded to the main hallway, I paused and did a quick check left and right to see who was around, when I saw a dark figure by the gym. I found out later it was Eric Harris. In that moment, he saw me as well and took three or four rapid-fire shots, penetrating into the wall just feet above my head! Bullets were ricocheting off of the lockers, and dust from the ceiling tiles was falling all around me. It felt like a war zone. I had nowhere to hide, and I was alone. *My fourth "fight for life". (Calamity Four)* Without even thinking, my body had already turned itself around, and I started to sprint. It's almost like cartoons, where characters are running in place but are not actually moving until they get enough traction. I remember sprinting back the same way I had just come from. My short time in the school was fortunately without serious physical consequences, even though I felt like I was being hunted down and was orchestrating my own escape.

At the time, I played on the high school football team for Columbine. We were always timing ourselves on our forty-yard dash to see who was the fastest. This was undoubtedly the fastest forty-yard dash of my entire life! In those moments running, I remember thinking through a few scenarios of what potentially could come my way. *He's going to shoot me in the back and kill me! I'm going to hear a shot, and then I am going to be dead! Or maybe he will shoot me, and I will become paralyzed. Then, he will come and kill me. Or he will wound me, and I will crawl around the corner, where he will still be able to chase me down and kill me.*

These were not particularly winning thoughts. In the moment, they were a pretty somber assessment of my chances, knowing I *was* going to get shot in the back and ultimately meet my death. However, with bullets whizzing by my ears when I saw Eric initially, you can see why I felt my chances of survival were diminishing rapidly. Fortunately, I started running around the corner toward the exit I had initially seen with the logjam of kids. It was a moment of sheer relief to see that all of those kids had shuffled out. I still had a chance! Though I hadn't been shot, I still had a lot of hallways to cover to get to the door.

Perhaps, without any intention, I was the "sacrificial lamb" of distraction that sent Eric on a detour, allowing all of those kids to actually get out. I will never know. I ran out the exit door and across the street to Leawood Park. There, I met up with a couple of hundred kids who were trying to figure out what was going on. I ran into my friend Ian, who was a football buddy. Everyone there was saying how this event was all we were going to talk about when we went back to class later that day. Obviously, we still had no idea of the magnitude of this event.

Though I had been running for my life, it still could have been much worse for me. I was lucky. I was blessed! Someone was looking out for me that day! I had escaped my own death. *Who would have imagined that this would not be the only time I would be hiding to save my life?* Truly, we had no concept of what was actually happening or the significance of how this would play out.

From there, we went to my friend Eric's home, which backed up to the park. I thought I should call my parents and let them know I was okay. At this point, I was not sure if it was Dylan or Eric who started shooting from across the street at a crowd of students in the park. I dropped the phone, disappointed and angry I had not connected with my mother, as the area of safety I thought I was in immediately felt unsafe, and I needed to keep running! I grabbed my friend Greg, and we jumped the fence into someone's backyard, putting something between us and the shooters. We continued to run, hopping more fences until we felt we were at a safe distance. Once Greg and I parted ways to our respective houses, my mind began a replay of what had just occurred. It was surreal. The impact of this experience was just beginning to unfold.

My friend Greg survived this moment with me, only to be killed in action during his second tour of duty in Iraq. Sadly, our freedoms come at a very high price, but we can still honor those who have lost their lives by continuing to stand up for our country. We will be forever grateful for his service. Thank you, USMC LCpl Greg Rund.

DORENE

My day at the school office was completely normal until the other secretary received a call from her husband. "Something strange is going on at Columbine. I heard an explosion, and now I see cop cars arriving. Have you heard from the Education Center of anything going on?" Up to this point, we had heard nothing; however, one of our office assistants suddenly received a phone call from her son, who was using the school pay phone (remember, this was 1999 and very few people had cell phones) to call his mother to let her know that someone in the school had a gun and was shooting at kids.

Ironically, Bruce had taken the week of April 20 off from work for vacation. The irony of this was that all vacation requests had to be submitted before the end of the previous year. This particular week had never been chosen before, but we were sure thankful he was home this year! I called Bruce to tell him about a dropped call I received from Tyler and briefed him about the other phone calls we had just received, as well as instructions from the school district to lock down our elementary school. Trevor arrived home while I'm on the phone with Bruce. I told them to turn on the news. "There has been a situation at your school. It will be on the news. I am not sure exactly what has happened, but all the neighboring schools are on lockdown. You must watch."

Tyler's delay in contacting us was agonizing, as by now it had been hours of waiting and wondering. In the meantime, I was at work and all of my friends whose children attended Columbine had now connected with their children. I had not. So, while I was trying to keep it together, in silent prayer and holding onto my faith, our office was in complete mayhem! Because the district had put all neighboring schools on lockdown, yet still allowed parents to pick up their students, all five lines of our phones were continually ringing, while we were trying to tend to parents. The fear on their faces when they came into the building was heart-wrenching in and of itself. It became our duty to serve the community on many levels that day, including setting up check-out tables and checking identification for the long line of anxious parents. We also needed to keep teachers calm and well-instructed on how to manage their classrooms without creating fear in the little ones. We had been trained for fire drills and tornado drills, but not for something like this.

BRUCE

Desperately, I was driving towards the school looking for Tyler. Of course, I was unable to get through any main streets due to barricades and police cars, so I went through some back streets, only to observe hundreds of kids flooding out the doors toward Clement Park, nearby. In hopes of spotting Tyler, I observed for a while, but couldn't get close enough, so I returned home. The neighborhood was in complete chaos, with police cars, emergency vehicles, sirens, helicopters, and to add to the mix, panicked parents looking for their children.

Trevor and I remained at home, eyes glued to the television in a state of disbelief and panic. It is difficult for the mind to register what the eyes are seeing when something like this has never crossed your radar before. Unable to sit and do nothing but watch (especially with Trevor repeatedly voicing his concern about Tyler being in the library every day at this time), I jumped in the car again in an attempt to get eyes on Tyler and bring him safely home. Again, I was unsuccessful. Neighbors were in the streets asking for information. Sadly, I had no answers for them.

TREVOR

Staring at the television in complete disbelief, I watched the news feed of what was happening at my school. I saw students running out of the building with their hands over their heads, surrounded by law enforcement. *How could this be happening? I was just there! I had passed Eric and Dylan in the parking lot as I was leaving! Why didn't they kill me then?* Reality set in. It was about this time that the words Eric Klebold spoke to me yesterday in the hallway, "Have a nice day tomorrow," really hit me. I flashbacked to a few hours earlier when I was leaving the school and heading for my car in the parking lot. I had seen both Dylan and Eric approach the school. Thank you God, that they did not see me in that moment! I could have easily been their first victim! My heart sank in the relief of that realization.

It seemed so surreal to me. My mind could not comprehend what was actually taking place. I could hear sirens flying by and see helicopters overhead. Then, the thought occurred to me that I would have still been there had the office not been so busy! Thank God for that detour! I remember feeling numb as shock began to set in.

I did have enough awareness in those numbing moments, however, to take concern about my brother, Tyler. *Where is Tyler?* Knowing full well this time of day was also his lunch and study hall break, I knew he spent this time in the library, *every day*! The news reports were explaining there were shootings in the library! They were showing footage of a sign in the library window pleading for help that read, "1 bleeding to death." Later, the footage continued with one student, Patrick Ireland, trying to escape out of the window with assistance from law enforcement. He had been shot in the head and was paralyzed on one side.

My body moved from a state of numbness to fight-or-flight mode for my brother. I had to choose both! I must "fly" back to school and "fight" to save the life of my brother, who was not of driving age and had no car. I couldn't just sit here and watch!

Columbine High School.

Columbine Memorial.

I called and spoke to my mother at work about my heroic plan. She became the voice of reason, explaining there was no way I would even be allowed close to the school. There was security everywhere!

My father arrived back home about this time and concurred with Mom. He had just been in the area and had to take a detour to get home. It was obvious to him something critical was going on at the school and was quite relieved to have me safe at home. One child is accounted for, but where was the other? "Is he in the library? It is the only place he goes during his study hall time. Is he able to escape the mayhem taking place? Did he try calling my mom from the library, and that is why the call was dropped? What is really going on?" These were the questions we were all asking. It felt like an out-of-body experience for all of us. It was as if we were watching this play out for someone else.

My concern for Tyler was giving way to anger, and I thought, "You know, I am going to rip him when I see him for not calling us for two hours!"

When Tyler finally arrived home with his friends, I was so relieved to lay eyes on him, my anger seemed to vanish immediately. There were no words. All I could do was give him a hug.

TYLER

When I arrived home several hours later, I found my dad and brother glued to the TV, watching the live news coverage of the shooting. Needless to say, they were both fixated on the events taking place at Columbine and so relieved to see I was safe and unharmed. Of course, I called my mom, who was still at her school, once I got home. She was beyond relieved to know I was okay, especially after the dropped call. For all she knew, I could have been a fatality.

Once it hit the news and became a national story, family and friends from all over the country began calling to see if Trevor and I were okay. It became an afternoon of telling the story and coming to terms with what had happened. I was just beginning to process it all. That night, and for many nights thereafter, I would have terrible nightmares of someone chasing me and trying to kill me. Over time, the dreams became less intense and less frequent as I continued to deal with what had happened on the day when history was transformed.

TREVOR

What was going to happen to me, to us, our senior class? We had waited for twelve years and worked hard for the last few months of our lives to celebrate being seniors and to experience the joy of that accomplishment. Someone had tried to take it away from us in the blink of an eye when we weren't looking and didn't expect it. Dylan and Eric had not only taken our school away, but they had also taken the thirteen lives that represented so many good and positive things our school stood for.

It was several days later when we received notice to come and claim any belongings left behind at Columbine. We were given a schedule of when to come to gather any backpacks we had left behind in a panic and lockers needed to be cleaned out. I remember sitting in the gym, patiently waiting our turn to be called. By groups, we were allowed to go to our lockers. This was such an eerie feeling. Then, I noticed the three bullet holes in my locker and the bullet holes and marks on the ceilings and walls surrounding it. It was a stark reminder our school had been turned into a war zone. Could these markings have been the result of the exact same bullets chasing Tyler down the hallway? We had been blessed to come out of this alive. Not everyone was as fortunate. It was then I also realized, I would never attend school here again. I can honestly say, I felt cheated.

The life, the energy, the learning, the teachers, the staff, the friendships, and the memories that were made here seemed to now hold such a bittersweet feeling. Shocked and completely unaware and unprepared for the emotional loss that would wash over us all, I slowly gathered my things from my locker with purposeful delay. I knew once I closed the door and reset the lock, I would never open it again. My heart felt heavy as I closed this chapter of my life.

From here, I could only wait in anticipation to watch how things would unfold and what was going to happen to the rest of my senior year. The decision was made that the offer from the principal of a neighboring high school

(Chatfield High) to open their doors to our student body and staff would be accepted. Finding out about Chatfield resulted in mixed feelings for me. Though I was relieved to know we had somewhere to go and completely understood the circumstances, I still felt like a castaway. The sensation of numbness was a blessing that helped me move through this time. While changes were happening around me, I was able to participate without taking on the emotions that come with being completely engaged. It was a means of survival and protection for me.

The school situation was strange at Chatfield. After all, we were rivals! No one knew what to say to each other. Kids were coming and going, passing each other in the hallways in an atmosphere filled with so many mixed emotions. The student body at Chatfield opened their doors to us with open arms, for which we were very grateful. We realized our being there was uncomfortable for them as well. Even though their student body attended in the morning, and ours in the afternoon, we had changed the energy in the school. Again, the normal high energy, excitement, celebrations, and feelings of accomplishments for their seniors had now been dampened by the energy we brought, of the loss and mourning in our hearts for the teacher and twelve students who were no longer a part of our lives.

Chatfield became a melting pot of so many mixed emotions to deal with by combining both student bodies. The highs, the lows, the love, the anger, the regrets, the sympathy, the lack of knowing how to carry on, the questions from both schools, and the dark cloud we felt we brought to them. It was very awkward for everyone. What else could we do? Where else could we go? We were thankful they opened their doors and their hearts to allow us to finish our year with them. Thank you, Chatfield High School!

In the end, it made our class stronger for it, and I hope it did the same for them as well. We have a special bond no one else can understand. I am not in the military, but I imagine it is like the bond that is shared between military families as well. It is an understanding of feelings and strength that never need to be spoken.

Shortly following our transition of schools, Lauren Townsend's mother came to speak to our class. She spoke about Lauren's prediction of her own death two weeks before it happened. She offered her phone number to the entire student body in support, if they ever needed to call. I remember her mother's strength and wisdom coming through her talk. The courage and compassion she displayed that day gave me hope that I, too, could be courageous and continue forward with a purposeful attitude. Ironically, I now work closely with Lauren's mother, as well as a classmate of Tyler's. Perhaps it is God's way of allowing her and I to heal on yet another level.

Lauren modeled the same behavior as her mother. She didn't speak a lot, but when she did, you were drawn to listen. Lauren and I didn't spend a lot of time together, but alphabetically for school functions, we were always next to each other in the sequence. When it was time for graduation exercises and practices, it was extremely difficult to not have her next to me, sharing chuckles and conversation. The day of graduation, her name would not be announced after mine. Her absence that day left me with a feeling of such emptiness, and yet I was supposed to be celebrating my graduation without her and without the others who were taken from us. It was an extremely difficult day.

LAUREN TOWNSEND
Excerpts from Lauren's Diary

A woman in the middle of a field of flowers kissing Jesus' wounds, I didn't think I could draw such a beautiful picture. I did tonight. It took me only two hours. I think something was guiding me other than just my hand. That is my dream. When I die, I want to wake up in a field of flowers and see Jesus there smiling, happy to see me, holding my hand. Then I want to kiss his wounds. Maybe it sounds corny, but I can't even describe how happy I would be if I could do that. Then I would hug him, he'd kiss me on the forehead, and we would just sit there hugging in the sun with the wind blowing our hair. The wind is God because God is everywhere. Just that moment is worth living many lives for.

I feel so peaceful, calm, and joyful, like I am on the verge of enlightenment. There is so much more going on here than we realize. I do think humanity is losing touch with itself and their relationship with their surroundings. Unfortunately it usually takes a huge trauma to get people to realize what is important and I feel that is what is going to happen to wake everyone up to get in touch with their spiritual sides. I am not afraid of death for it is only a transition. For, in the end all there is, is love.

These words by Lauren Townsend, who lost her life during the shooting, are found at the Columbine Memorial.

Graduation day itself left me feeling incomplete about my high school years. My emotions around it seemed very neutral. I just didn't allow myself to feel anything surrounding that day. Perhaps it was a way of protecting myself from a complete meltdown. It seemed the day also came with a Hollywood production for the national media to view. I remember feeling some resentment toward the media and journalists. It felt as if they were exploiting us by requesting interviews and stories to sensationalize our experiences. I realize the nation was grieving right along with us; however, we all knew that, from the public eye, our school and community had now been tainted with an inaccurate perspective about all of us. We just wanted to remain the unassuming, quiet little community we once knew.

All of this seemed to smother our graduation celebration. We were all still mourning, so the graduation seemed to hold very little value to me. Not at all the exciting end to the senior year I had once anticipated and had looked so forward to for so many years.

REFLECTION

As time passed, it was revealed to the community there had been an adult prayer group at Columbine High School. They prayed weekly for the safety and protection of our school. You might say to yourself,

"Well, obviously those prayers weren't heard, or all of these lives would not have been taken. Where was God today?"

Here is where God was: He was busy guarding the bombs that were set to go off in the cafeteria. After the investigations began, it was discovered for some "unexplained" reason, the numerous bombs which should have exploded, remained completely intact. There was no physical explanation as to why there were not multiple explosions in the cafeteria. The attempt to take the lives of many more students and staff had been snuffed out. That's where God was. So now you might ask, "Why were any lives taken then?"

We are not always given the answers to each moment but are still asked to praise God in *all* things, even the things we don't understand at the time. We do know, however, this event touched the lives of every community member in some way, and God will bring good out of even the worst situations.

Moving Forward

The Columbine High School Massacre, April 20, 1999, at the time, was the deadliest school shooting in America.

A total of thirteen deaths, twelve students (ten of which were killed in the library), and one teacher and twenty-four injured. The perpetrators committed suicide, making it fifteen deaths in total.

TYLER

So, what do I still keep with me today? I will always have sympathy for the families who don't have a brother, a sister, or a father because they were lost on such a catastrophic day and how their lives must still be affected by the loss from this tragedy. It makes you realize how quickly life can be taken away or changed. The hundreds of families who sent their sons and daughters off to school on April 20 were certainly not thinking there would be a chance they would not return home. You just never know when your time is up. Whether a death is anticipated or unexpected, life is fragile and precious. You need to welcome it; you need to try to live every day to its fullest. I have learned not to hold a grudge because you never know about tomorrow. You may not be able to remedy a situation or take back words you may come to regret, as it was the last thing you said to someone.

I still take away the fact that, if you have never been in a similar situation or found yourself in an unexpected event, there is no 20/20 vision lookup. Sometimes people like to offer their suggestions of what they would have done had they been in my shoes. For instance, "I would have gone after the gunman." That's all well and good after the fact, but in the fog of war, if you will, the intensity in the moment causes you to react on minimal information. You find yourself moving instinctively in order to stay out of harm's way. I didn't have a gun to go after him anyway. It is very easy to armchair quarterback what you would or could have done differently. However, most of those hypotheticals are not going to hold up in those highly stressful situations of unknowns. One should think first, before judging another's response. This would especially hold true with any first responders as well, who are risking their lives for the sake of others.

As the healing process continued for several weeks following, many people remained curious to know everyone's story. Police investigations required a detailed account of each student's experience. People outside of the student body and staff were trying to offer and show support during such a difficult time. I remember getting really angry because they tried to explain how they understood. In fact, they didn't! They couldn't! They weren't there! I thought to myself, "You absolutely do not and cannot know what it was like!" So, I began to close off to people who weren't there, who couldn't share in what had happened that day.

Eventually, the school was providing counselors for anyone who wanted to take part. Finally, after some prodding from my family, we made an appointment. Of course, the counselor came to help me understand the words of others I found so offensive were, in fact, just words. In reality, their intentions were genuine. This is an important lesson to share. When others are expressing themselves, it is more important to listen to their *heart* than to their *words*.

I also learned, and still hold with me, how I deal with stressful situations. In fact, when I was forced to eject out of my aircraft over combat territory in Libya, I once again faced the challenge of facilitating my own rescue.

TREVOR

When I hear of similar news events of more mass killings, I find myself not able to turn off the television as I am connecting with their experience and hoping they come through it. How does one move on with this? Through the assistance of counseling, I acquired some new skills in dealing with my anger and frustration. Also, in understanding how important it is to let go of the things one can't control. Resentment prevents you from moving forward.

I walked away with a new focus on myself and realized how this had changed me as a person. It taught me to value life at a whole different level and to search out the positive pieces in my relationships. It has helped me appreciate the things around me I once may have taken for granted. Whether it is people, nature, my simple lifestyle, a song, or a kind word spoken to me, the gratitude comes much easier.

Try not to take any of your days for granted. Life is filled with highs and lows, which may frustrate you and take your focus away from your family and loved ones. Be welcoming to others as well because you never know when or how you will make a difference in a life. A smile, a simple good morning, can never be overrated. Always be willing to acknowledge others for what they do and recognize their positive attributes and efforts. As you bless, so shall you be blessed.

I now understand, life can change in a moment and should not be taken for granted. The next day may not be the same as today. For some, tomorrow may not come. It also changed my future focus, my purpose, my life path. I decided to turn to Human Development in search of ways to help others who had also experienced tragedy and despair. I want to make a difference in the lives of others, to give them tools to rise above their disappointments and challenges, to help them become the best they can be. Perhaps this will give them some hope to overcome. There are circumstances where trauma in a young person's life can be completely blocked out of the conscious mind. However, the memory may never goes away. It's a matter of how deep the events are pushed down and how one can manage to find normalcy in their life over time.

Be kind and compassionate to one another, forgiving each other, just as in Christ, God forgave you.

EPHESIANS 4:32

Forgiveness does not imply that offensive behavior is condoned or acceptable. It simply means you are releasing the offense. An open wound will continue to fester inside without proper care. This also holds true for our emotions and our spirit.

DORENE

Unfortunately, for the seniors of Columbine, most would continue to struggle. Having lost their teacher and classmates and then banished from their school, the grieving was quite intense for them. Students took ownership and loyalty of their school and what it stands for. The normal high school celebrations of closing out those long awaited twelve years had now been shattered. Sports and other activities could no longer be played on "home soil." For the most part, these kids expressed feeling a sense of homelessness. Columbine High School was part of their identity. It was a highly respected and desirable school in academics as well as sports, and now, to those on the outside, two students, Eric Harris and Dylan Klebold, as well as the media, had redefined it.

Tragically, it would only be the beginning of many more changes to come. The entire community felt wounded by this event, but collectively, we were committed to rise above this with the support of one another, so as not to allow this to permanently tarnish our lives or neighborhoods. *United we stand, divided we fall.*

Time passed, and Trevor and Tyler appeared to be doing as well as could be expected, even though we knew the impact would have lasting effects. So, reverting to prayer once again, I inquired to God as to how they were *really* doing under the masks they were wearing. Well, true to His promise, He answers . . . in His time.

Post-Traumatic Stress Disorder (PTSD)

The Fourth of July was approaching, so we thought a family night out at the baseball game and viewing fireworks sounded like a great way to celebrate! It was a lovely Colorado summer evening with the family together, sharing time and enjoying a great display of fireworks. All is good for the moment until suddenly, as we were exiting the stadium, a "misfire" occurred, and there was a loud blast. In the blink of an eye, Tyler was gone! We didn't see him anywhere. Once again, without the availability of cell phones, there was no way to communicate. The best hope we had was to "divide and conquer."

Bruce and Trevor made their way to the car on high alert, while I remained standing guard where we last saw him in hopes of his return. Those thirty minutes felt like a lifetime when there was no knowledge of what was taking place. During that "lifetime," I prayed again. (It was now becoming a constant practice.) Shortly thereafter . . . relief! He resurfaced!

"What happened to you? Where did you go?" I asked.

"I am not really sure, Mom. When I heard the blast, my feet just took off. I didn't even realize I was running until I looked around. I didn't know where I was, and my family was nowhere to be seen. I figured my best bet was to just turn around and go back, hoping you would wait for me."

Once again, God had answered my question: Our children were not doing as well as they appeared or as well as we had hoped. This would be especially true for Tyler. There was obviously some post-traumatic stress with the sounds of unexpected explosions, which was certainly understandable. Not being sure where to turn for help, more prayers were in order.

During this time, I had been seeing a chiropractor who had just remodeled his clinic for expansion and then, a week later, abruptly quit his practice and moved out of state. It was so abrupt, even the office staff was not prepared. I found this to be a bit strange; however, once again it was by divine design. Chiropractors are not in short supply in Colorado, but how would I find just the right one amongst so many? Again, turning to guess whom? Yes, I went straight to the Divine! The message I heard was, of all things, "Go to the phone book." I thought, "You have got to be kidding me. The Yellow Pages? That's like a needle in a haystack!" Needless to say, off I went to grab the phone book. By this time, I had learned not to question, even when it didn't make sense. *Trust.*

Here is where *obedience* would play out, showing me the guidance I needed. I thought I would narrow down the selection by demographics. I knew *what* I was looking for, just not *who*. With questions in one hand, phone book in the other, I began my search. I know this sounds like a fiction story sometimes, but it is written in truth. I read each name of the listed doctors out loud, asking for a "nudge" to alert me when I came to the correct one. It was Foothills Chiropractic that came with the nudge, so I picked up the phone and began with my questions.

On the day of my appointment, I drove up to the address and honestly was a little disappointed. It turned out, the office was nothing more than a small cinderblock building with only four parking spaces. I came with no expectations, or so I thought, but the first impression was a bit sketchy. Nonetheless, I felt I was led there, so I was not going to question it any further. I walked in and noted the inside was as basic as the outside; however, the woman at the desk was welcoming and invited me to take a seat.

As I was waiting, wondering what this experience was going to reveal, I looked on the wall, where there were some brochure holders, and noticed one of them gave information on Neuro Emotional Technique (NET). As I began to read the pamphlet, I was completely captivated by the explanation of how this technique could be used to modify emotional trigger points in the body as well as Post Traumatic Stress Disorder (PTSD). Chills ran through my body as I thought about our two sons and how I had asked for God's guidance in helping them heal. I now understood why God removed my previous doctor. I thought I was searching for a new doctor for myself. In actuality, God was leading me to a place of healing for our sons. I chuckled to myself upon the realization of what just occurred. It is so intentional how God moves us in the direction we need to go, if we are asking and willing to be obedient. Here is a great example of why we need to know what we are asking for and why we are asking for it. Then we are able to recognize where it came from, our responsibility for what we do with it. This is also why God asks us to praise him in *all* things, even when it may not make sense to us. He always knows exactly what is going on.

———⌒———

Oh, put God to the test and see how kind he is!
See for yourself the way his mercies shower down
on all who trust in him. If you belong to the Lord,
reverence him; for everyone who does this
has everything he needs. Even strong young lions
sometimes go hungry, but those of us who reverence
the Lord will never lack any good thing.

PSALM 34:8 -10 TLB

———————

In this moment, the appearance of this building was completely dismissed from my initial misjudgment. I now knew I was in just the right place! I was more than pleased with my appointment, which also included a nice conversation around this NET modality which I had never previously heard about. As it turns out, Dr. John Fisher was a Vietnam vet who had returned to his home soil with severe PTSD. It was through the path of trying to heal himself that he came to know about this technique. He has written several fiction books and travels to Vietnam frequently to treat and assist the people living in the villages there.

Of course, I brought the pamphlet home and talked to the family about this new discovery. Both boys decided they had nothing to lose in giving it a try, so try it they did. After a series of sessions with the "master" of NET, Trevor expressed that, indeed, it was "the best gift we could have ever given him." Tyler also felt it made a difference for him as well, but not sure of the degree. He decided to wait and see how things would settle. Now years later, while the memories remain, the PTSD does not. How good is God?

REFLECTION

It is noteworthy here for any of you who have been through a traumatic event or have suffered a loss of any kind, there is hope for your healing. The most important thing to realize is that holding onto an emotion of *any* kind can negatively affect your physical health over time. Your physical ailments are simply your body's only way of communicating to you that there is an emotional component you may need to address and clear away.

This *is not* a form of years of counseling. It is in fact, a way of helping your body become congruent with the emotions giving you resistance. The sessions typically are not lengthy, nor should they be costly, even without the assistance of insurance, which will not cover the costs of this treatment. The number of sessions necessary will vary with each individual.

If you feel this caught your attention and resonates with you, I urge you to research your area for a chiropractor who uses Applied Kinesiology in conjunction with the NET application. Applied Kinesiology taps into your mind. Your mind knows exactly what you are holding, where you are holding the negative energy, and why. This is an amazing tool for healing. Give yourself the hope and healing that is available to you and that you so deserve. It can potentially change your life!

MY HEART BEGAN TO POUND OUTSIDE OF MY CHEST, AND PANIC BEGAN TO RISE AGAIN. I HAD TO STAY CALM IF I WANTED TO STAY ALIVE.

chapter seven

THE HUNT

Who would have imagined this horrific day at Columbine would not be the only time I would be hiding for my life, with that feeling of someone chasing and trying to kill me? This time, however, I'm in Libya—a long way from home . . . and alone.

TYLER

I did a quick look around to see if by some miracle MeSo had landed close. I didn't see anything and I didn't have time to look for him. We are trained not to spend any time, energy, or effort looking for a crewmate as it takes away from the primary mission of evading. Everyone is trained to be a survivor/evader as a singleton. Of course, the parachute had tangled up in the thorn bush I narrowly escaped upon landing. I quickly reached for the parachute knife in my G-suit pocket . . . it wasn't there! *Really?*

I tried untangling the parachute but did not want to spend too much time where I was. I knew I needed to move and find a hiding spot to gather my wits and come up with a plan. I pulled the raft and parachute close to me, unzipped the hit-and-run kit, and started to detach the seat kit from the raft. I had never done this in training, but it should be easy. Right? Well, at night, with my adrenaline pumping, I couldn't immediately figure out the non-standard clasp, so I set the kit down to use two hands. As I freed the seat kit, I started to hear noises. This was taking way too long, and panic was rising. The instant the seat kit was free, I bolted, accidentally leaving behind the hit-and-run kit.

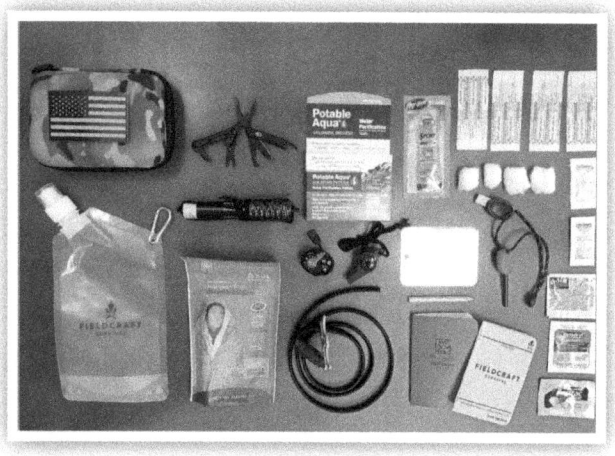

Escape kit.

My next moves were to find somewhere to hide and to drink some of the water pouches in our survival kit. In training they drilled into us that initial hydration is crucial to help limit symptoms of shock from the ejection.

I hobbled about eighty yards from where I landed to a medium-size thornbush that provided minimal cover, but it was all I had. After all, I was in the desert. After forty-five seconds, I found the water in my vest pocket, which I was unaware I had. This comes back to me not being familiar with a fully packed combat vest and its contents.

As I crawled under the bush, I got out the CSEL (Combat Survivor Evader Locator) radio and began the process of contacting rescue forces and assessing my surroundings. About half a mile away, I could see the crash and a major road between me and the crash site. To my right was a small shed, to my left a larger house – both were several hundred yards away. Behind me was a two-lane road with rolling hills beyond it. I was thankful it was a full moon that night, with just a few clouds. This made things a bit easier, as I rarely had to use the flashlight, which would have drawn more attention to myself.

I remember watching the jet burn. It took about thirty minutes before the fire finally died. It was surreal seeing the jet I was just flying in engulfed in flames while I was trying to evade for my life. I did not have a grand plan at that point. My mind was still reeling and processing the reality of landing on the ground in Libya. I actually was *alive*! The training kicked in even with the brain fog I was experiencing.

The CSEL radio was very new at the time. We were the first F-15E unit to fly with it in combat. We had received some training, via PowerPoint, but minimal hands-on training. Of course, I had paid attention to the brief, but, at that time, I thought, *I won't ever need to use this as I don't ever plan on ejecting! That will never happen to me, and if it does, I am sure I can figure it out when I need to. It seems easy enough, and I am good with electronics.* Now, I was right in the middle of the unexpected!

I initiated the radio, which started getting the GPS fixed on my location and going through several pro-grammed questions like, "Are you hurt? Can you move? Are there hostile forces in the area?" At the end of the questions, it required authentication. In the event enemy forces found the radio, they would be unable to signal recovery forces into a trap. Usually, it is a letter in the word of the day.

Part of our special instructions included a color, letter, and word of the day. These changed on a daily basis, and we were briefed as we stepped to the jet. This informa-tion could not be written down but must be memorized. Unfortunately, as a result of the chaos (due to our rapid departure) and lack of information early on, when we stepped to our aircraft our intel briefed us one word of the day; however, the white board, with all the applicable information, had a different word of the day. I noticed it but was so oversaturated in other things I did not query which one was correct.

The CSEL prompted me for the third letter of the word of the day, I must have guessed wrong. After complet-ing the initial "call for help," I got a timely message back asking, "What's your callsign?" I thought they knew the radio was paired to me when it was activated, and so I gave them my personal callsign, Mask. I would find out later that they wanted the flight callsign and position, Bolar 34B.

After I sent my personal callsign, I needed to move and find a better hole-up site. The problem was my knee. It was killing me. I could barely put weight on it, causing me to move at a slow hobble. All the training we did, which was challenging enough, was without any injuries. Now, I had a bum knee complicating my evasion.

As I exited my first hole-up site, I felt a little better. I had made contact and rescue forces at least knew I was alive and on the ground. Or so I thought. I shed my harness and my G-suit and tossed them in a bush. We had desert gear, flight suit, boots etc., since we were flying over a desert, but they only make one color G-suit, which is army green. I wanted to be as camouflaged as possible, even at night. Before I took my G-suit off, I checked the pockets to make sure I wasn't leaving anything. Ha! I found a can of dip that I had left in my G-suit pocket as well as a piece of candy! I grabbed them and the flashlight I had borrowed from Boozer. Surprisingly, both had remained in my G-suit through the ejection even though I had not zipped the pockets. Lucky me!

Still on a search for a better hole-up site, I noticed a large thornbush down a rolling hill away from the main roads and farther away from the house I had spotted. I hobbled another eighty to ninety yards, trying to stay quiet and low to not be silhouetted by the bright light of the moon. When I got to my second hole-up site, I began to dig out the bottom of the bush a little to reduce my profile. Since hitting the ground, I heard flight lead, Bolar 33, overhead, doing shows of force as low as they could go, which was limited to ten thousand feet. As I was getting established in the hole-up site, they did another show of force and put out flares, ensuring that anyone in the area knew there was a jet overhead, hopefully deterring any hostiles. I had been making a little noise getting deep into the bush and started to hear a dog barking, but I had no idea how far away it was. It was close enough to be aware of, but not close enough for immediate concern.

As quietly as I could, I took out the CSEL radio and read a message: "Stay where you are; help is on the way." I assumed everything had worked as expected—that my location had been sent to the JPRC (Joint Personnel Recovery Center), and the info was being relayed to Bolar 33 overhead. I didn't use the radio mode of the CSEL as any noise drew the attention of the dogs. What I forgot about was the headphones. I would have to have made minimal radio calls to hide my noise signature, but at least, I would have been able to follow what was going on with MeSo and any other aircraft overhead. Instead, I could only rely on text messages, of which there were none.

As it turns out, it wouldn't have made any difference for me. My radio was programmed incorrectly, and instead of the message going to JPRC at Rammstein Air Base in Germany, where they were aware of the missions in Libya, they went to the default location at Tyndall AFB in Florida. They had little, if any, idea of what missions were being flown in Libya, by whom and where they were. Additionally, the radio was programmed to look for GPS, and if it did not find it, it would turn off the GPS antennae to save battery. The batteries were rated for about twelve hours of GPS/radio use, and we carried a spare battery. The software turned out not to be user-friendly. I had to delve three menus deep to check my fix or location. It simply stated how old your last GPS fix was, but there was no indication on the top-level menu. If I would have checked my fix, it would have said three-days old, and the location would have been RAF Lakenheath, UK, when they verified the radios worked. That was the location that Tyndall AFB received. Never did they request an updated fix.

I assumed, with good coordinates passed to those overhead and signaling devices out, they would quickly find my location and start the rescue forces rolling. I felt a little bit of comfort "knowing" help was on the way. Or so I thought.

Knowing that Bolar 33 was overhead, I wanted to signal my position in hopes they would see me in their NVGs as well as cueing in the targeting pod. Again, not knowing where things were in the combat vest stung me, and I had to go through multiple pockets to find the firefly, 9V batteries, and the IR chemstick. As I dug through my vest, I made noise, and a dog started to approach my position. I went motionless for a few minutes so that the dog would go away and I could continue to search my vest. This back and forth happened four or five times, extending the time it took to get out the signaling devices. At one point, the dog got so close, I could tell it was a medium-to-large-sized dog with long hair. It probably was a sheep dog, since I had also seen a couple of sheep in the distance. The dog got so close that I started reaching for my gun in case it attacked me. A barking dog might draw a tiny bit of attention; a gunshot would surely draw maximum attention! I sure was hoping I would not have to use my gun. Eventually, I found the firefly and 9V batteries and placed them just outside the bush alongside a rock. Then, I realized I needed to pee; actually, I had to pee since we had taken off almost five hours ago. But yeah, that was how my day was going! With the dog distracted by a car in the distance and no other movement, I rolled to one side, almost taking a knee, and finally going. Immediate relief!

By now, at least ninety minutes had passed. I knew that with my mobility limited, I could actually be there for some time, so I needed to develop a long-term plan. The hole-up site I was in was okay for the night but would not suffice at sunrise. The only direction free from threats was behind me, across the road, and up the hills away from the crash site, where eventually people would surely gather, and away from the houses and dog. It was several hundred yards to the top of the hills with little protection, so timing my movement would be critical.

I wasn't running *to* anything. I was simply hoping there would be a better hole-up site on the other side. Since I didn't know exactly where I was going, I could very well be exposed. The moon was up and in the same direction as the hills. I didn't want to be hobbling along and silhouetted in moonlight as I made my way up. By now, a car was passing every five to ten minutes. I was waiting for my gap, where the moon was behind clouds and the road was clear. The feelings of isolation, frustration, and abandonment would wash over me from time to time, and the thought, *What am I doing here in Libya, at night, by myself, trying not to get captured? I don't belong here, now engaging in my fifth fight for life! (Calamity Five)*

My plan was to find a new hole-up site, continue to communicate through text, and wait for recovery. I was mentally preparing myself to be there through the next morning. Remembering what time the sun rose in England, I knew I had around five hours before I had to be on the move and find a more robust and secure hole-up site somewhere else. As I was waiting for my window of opportunity, I started to hear movement and commotion from the field I originally landed in—faint voices and at least one vehicle. I was hoping they would not find the parachute and raft, even though I knew they were not hidden. I stayed absolutely still to avoid drawing attention to my location. In the distance, I saw a truck, with its headlights off, rolling to a stop.

I heard several voices, and while I don't speak Arabic, the voices did not seem agitated or hostile, but almost matter of fact. "We found a parachute." Though their voices did not have any excitement in them, my adrenaline was surging. My heart began to pound outside of my chest, and panic began to rise again. I had to stay calm if I wanted to stay alive. This was the closest anyone had been to my location. I didn't hear any radios, just two different male voices. I was hoping they would continue on their way. I didn't have an immediate feeling of fear, but one of trepidation, since I was uncertain of their intent. My gut was telling me these guys were not Gaddafi or his men, but I didn't know who they were and didn't want to find out. I thought about defending myself, contemplating at what point I was going to start shooting.

Many guys talked about pulling their radio and gun out of the holster while they were still under canopy if people were around. This gave them some options, rather than being captured. They would shoot their way out if able or take down as many as they could before they were killed. I remembered what my ROTC commander said in 2006, that he would shoot himself before he would allow himself to get captured. Unlike my ROTC commander, I was not in that frame of mind. I still had options. I was going to get out of there.

After the very short exchange between the two men, I heard the truck start up and begin moving, getting louder as they approached my position. They finally stopped only thirty yards away. I hugged the ground even tighter, thought "thin," and focused on controlling my breathing. For me, this was a high stakes game of hide and seek! The truck doors opened. Within moments, a search light was sweeping the field around and over me, lighting up the top of the bush and passing on. I thought

I might be safe. But as the light swept back in my direction, it reached the bush again and stopped. And so did my heart! A sinking feeling washed over me as I tried to remain as quiet and as still as possible. I knew I was on the brink of being discovered. *Maybe they see me, maybe they don't, but I'm about to find out.*

"Hey, American, you can come out. It's okay!" The accent was American, which kind of surprised me, and for some reason, I didn't feel as threatened as I expected. Still, I was not giving up that easily, so I continued to stay motionless. After about fifteen seconds I hear the voice again. "Hey American, come out; we will not hurt you." Facing the light with my head down in the desert dirt, I heard footsteps slowly approaching from my right side. Sheep? Dog? Person? As the sound increased, it was clear the footsteps were human. Then I heard another set of steps. I was being approached from two different directions, not in a searching pattern. Both were headed straight for me. As they got within ten to fifteen feet, I began to panic and knew that any sudden movement might be interpreted as a hostile act if they got any closer. I had heard plenty of automatic gunfire throughout the night and did not want to risk getting shot. I knew there was literally nothing else around me as far as hiding spots. They knew where I was!

As I stood up, I feared the unknown, but "something" was giving me peace of mind that these individuals were not necessarily hostile or threatening. We practiced getting found by local civilians in SERE training, and the tone and feel was the same as in training. I walked towards the light initially with my hands up, saying, "Okay, okay." As I walked out of the beam of the search light toward the man who was calling out, I looked back at the bush. It had no foliage on it, and you could see right through it. Not a good hole-up site at all, but it was the best I had. As I approached the man and the truck, a feeling of dread and fear washed over me, as the realization of being captured became all-consuming.

They have me.

chapter eight

CAPTURED

———⌇———

"Fear not, for I am with you;
Be not dismayed, for I am your God.
I will strengthen you, Yes, I will help you."

ISAIAH 41:10 NKJV

———

The First Phone Call

TYLER

As I got closer to the truck, I saw a middle-aged man walking to meet me and an overweight man behind him, while another person approached from my right. I could see he was younger, maybe mid-twenties with an AK-47. We met in-between the truck and the bush. The man at the truck called himself "the Colonel" and was dressed in a mix of military clothing and business attire. He told me he wanted to help. As we approached the truck, I heard a distinct jet noise, different than it had been the entire night. Originally, I thought it was Bolar 33, but by this time, they had reached BINGO fuel and had to go to the tankers to get more gas. It was Viper flight—two F-16s providing coverage while Bolar 33 was getting refueled. Since I wasn't on the radio, I didn't know what was about to happen. But I had heard that distinct jet sound before.

A couple of years ago in training, I volunteered to be a bad guy on the ground so other F-15E aircrews could practice close air support. (Interesting, I chose *that* role!) The sound was a jet rolling into strafe (which is to shoot the guns of the aircraft towards the ground with rapid fire in order to appear like a wall of bullets). Though I didn't process soon enough at the time, I was still processing the fact I was just "rolled-up" (captured). Before I could think about it anymore, just past the truck about forty yards from our location, a thundering clatter and a twenty-foot-tall wall of white and orange explosions lit up the night. My immediate thought was they were shooting at us and had missed.

The larger man who was between us and the truck, only ten yards away, turned around, grasping his bleeding head. He has been hit by some of the incendiary rounds. There was panic between the three men as they hollered, "Call the jets off, call the jets off! We are here to help you!"

Now, we heard a wingman's jet start to roll in. Everyone around me dove to the ground to take cover. I remember very clearly thinking, *So far, today had been a bad day.* A spin, an ejection, multiple parachute issues, injuring my knee, getting captured, and now being shot at. I didn't know if they were trying to strafe us or not, but if they were going to shoot us, laying down wasn't going to help. Running in any direction might put me in the line of fire so I stood there thinking, *If today is the day, then there is nothing I can do about it.* Thankfully, the wingman was farther away, and we were fine. When they stood up again, they looked at me a little like I was crazy and a little like I was fearless. At that point, I just wanted to be home. They asked me again what they could do to help, and in that tense moment, I was still not sure if they were truly friendly or playing along to make me think they were.

We were taught in our training—*do not trust.* I knew the rebel uprising was in Benghazi, and while they were not American or even NATO forces, they were surely the friendliest forces in the country. My litmus test on whether they were actually friend or enemy was to ask them to take me to Benghazi. They quickly agreed, and we got in the car. While I didn't process it fully at the time, they never asked me to surrender my gun throughout them initially finding me and the "stressful" walk to the truck. A good indicator they were truly willing to help.

Once in the truck, which was about the same size as a 1985 Chevy S-10 pickup, my place was between the Colonel and the large man that was wounded in the strafe. The younger man with the AK-47 was standing in the bed of the truck. As we left the site where they found me, they were very cautious, trying not to draw attention, so they would turn their headlights off on the dirt roads when they were straight and then back on for a corner, then back off once we were through the turn. The Colonel was making several calls, all in Arabic. I was hoping he was calling to clear our path to Benghazi, but for all I knew he could have been talking to Gaddafi!

We drove for about ten minutes, then approached a small village. There was a lot of excitement and around twenty people. Most of the attention was on a car that had clearly just arrived, and they were taking someone who had been injured out of the car. The two men in the car started to get angry and blame me for the injury to the individuals. They were saying it was the jets that were trying to hurt them, and I needed to call them off. We only stayed in the village for about a minute then continued on. It was at this point, I continued to tell them I could not talk to the aircraft overhead. I did decide it was a good time to break radio silence and let anyone that might be listening know what my current situation was.

I was not sure what callsign I should use on the radio. (I would later find out, in this circumstance, you use your flight callsign, Bolar 34, and your position in the jet, either Alpha for the pilot or Bravo for the WSO, so I should have used Bolar 34B.) I knew you could give your captor your name. So, I decided to use that. "Any radio, any radio, this is Captain Tyler Stark. I am in a truck with three people, going to Benghazi." I heard the WSO from our flight lead answer, "Bolar 34B, this is Bolar 33. Confirm you are in a truck with people *talking on the radio*."

The second half of his statement was said in a slightly sarcastic and accusatory tone. He was subtly telling me I should not be using the radio in such proximity to someone whose ultimate intent was unknown to me. What Bolar 33 was attempting to do was give me a chance to use the duress word of the day, part of the SPINS, to determine whether I was held against my will. Since I thought I was in the wrong, I simply said, "Bolar 34B out." The crew of Bolar 33 now at least knew I was alive and where I was headed.

I relayed my impression that the radio was not going to help call off the jets to the men in the truck, and we continued on. After we got farther from the village, I could see the sky glowing from two big cities in the distance. I did not know what direction we were going but was confident one of them was Benghazi and the other was Ajdabiya. However, I didn't know which light in the distance was which. I assumed we were going mostly westerly, and the lights to the north were Benghazi and the lights to the south were Ajdabiya.

This was what I did know. Heading to Benghazi meant I would be going toward sympathetic, if not friendly, forces in the form of the rebels. Ajdabiya meant Gaddafi! This knowledge was based on the intel brief we got before we flew our mission. As we started to make our way closer to the southern lights, I thought I might need to escape if we didn't turn to a more northerly route.

My options were limited as I was in the middle of two of them, with the man with the AK-47 in the bed of the truck. *I needed an escape plan!* The plan I came up with, if it was clear they were Gaddafi sympathizers, was to reach over the large man to my right, open the door, push him out, and have him break my fall as we were driving. Once on the ground, I would pull out my gun and shoot the young man in the back with the confusion that would ensue. Then, it would be me and the Colonel, with the large man wounded from falling out of a moving truck. Maybe I had seen too many action movies, but that was my plan, and I began to mentally rehearse the actions should I have to take them. As I was mentally preparing for the James Bond escape, we pulled up to a derelict-looking building and stopped. I knew at this moment my grand escape plan was no longer going to work, since we had arrived at their destination.

They led me up a set of stairs off to the side of the building. As the door opened, they led me into the building, where I could see an open door at the end of a long hallway. Immediately, I saw the hallway was crowded with fifteen to twenty people. As they led me toward the crowd, many started taking pictures and videos with their cellphones. I initially hid my face so people could not take my photo until I remembered it was good to get your face out there to confirm that you were at least alive to any US forces. I raised my face and allowed them to take pictures.

Looking past the crowd, I could see we were headed toward a large room, where there was a half-circle of elderly looking individuals awaiting my arrival. This meeting was clearly what the Colonel had been arranging when he was on the phone in the truck. My heart started pounding, as I knew one of two things awaited me in the room—a friendly welcome or this was where the beatings and interrogations would begin. I could not immediately tell which scenario awaited me, but as I entered the room, they began clapping. It became clear to me that they were there to help.

I was overcome with relief as they welcomed me and continued to say, "thank you" for the US Air Force and our support against Gaddafi. They were convinced that the US support, at the right moment, had kept Gaddafi out of Benghazi. To them, I was their hero. Honestly, I felt the same toward them. They offered me juice and a biscuit, which I gratefully accepted.

---

*"Blessed is the one whom God corrects;
so do not despise the discipline of the Almighty.
For he wounds, but he also binds up; he injures,
but his hands also heal. From six calamities he will
rescue you; in seven no harm will touch you."*

JOB 5:17-19

After a few minutes, a gentleman walked in and identified himself as Habib. He was initially confused when
he was introduced to me, as he had been told a French
pilot had gone down. He said he was there to take me
the rest of the way to Benghazi. Shortly after the intro-
ductions were complete, Habib took me to his SUV. I said
goodbye to the Colonel and expressed my deepest gratitude to him and his friends for their help. We hopped
into Habib's SUV, with me in the back seat in an effort
to hide me. While my handoff was by all definitions
friendly, I was still not comfortable with fully trusting
anyone I was around. I tried to send a message using the
CSEL radio of my current situation and ultimate destination: "Going to Benghazi, please advise."

After multiple attempts using the text-messaging
capability of the radio, I still had no response. As we got
closer and closer to Benghazi, it was clear the security
around the city was more intense the closer you got.
We went through an outer checkpoint that had only a
few people with automatic weapons, AK-47s. As we got
closer, the frequency of the checkpoints increased, as
did the number of guards and armament they carried.
The fourth and final checkpoint was guarded by about a
dozen men with small- and large-caliber machine guns,
as well as guns mounted in the back of pickup trucks and
multiple RPGs.

Once cleared through the last checkpoint, I heard gunfire not ten feet away. I thought we were getting shot at!
Habib saw my reaction in the rearview mirror and told

me it was just the way the guard was welcoming us back into the city, by shooting an AK-47 straight into the air.

We pulled up to a hotel and stopped at the main entrance, where a valet would normally pick up your car. No valets. Instead, a small group of people stood there to welcome us. As soon as I got out of the car, an older man was the first to greet me. He offered me a rose, which I thought was a weird gift. I initially said thanks but no thanks. After all, I was a fighter pilot. Wanting to get home and walking around with a rose was just kind of weird. The man persisted, and Habib explained he was just trying to show his gratitude for the US's help, and he saw me as an unofficial representative of the US military. I took the rose with acknowledgement, and we continued walking into the lobby of the hotel.

The architecture and interior design looked like it was from the 1980s. You could tell that back in the day, when it was new, it was a very nice hotel. It had clearly not been updated or well maintained in quite some time. It looked very run down. About fifteen to twenty people met us in the lobby, a mix of civilians and what looked to be rebels with automatic weapons, dressed in paramilitary gear. Most of them were standing around the perimeter of the lobby. It felt like they were there to ensure security, primarily mine!

Three individuals walked up to me as I entered the main area of the lobby and identified themselves as Egyptian doctors who had come to Libya to provide medical assistance to the rebels and civilians who were fighting against Gaddafi. The taller bald man identified himself as an orthopedic surgeon; the woman, who had kind of a Cleopatra thing going on, was a cardiologist; and the shorter gentlemen was a general physician. After they had introduced themselves, the older man who had given me the rose came back up to me and started asking pointed questions about the US military's involvement.

He asked where we were flying out of, what our targets were, and what our mission details were. This took me a little off guard. Everything that had happened up to this point made me feel more and more comfortable and trusting of the people that were helping me. No one had asked any questions that might be considered sensitive. My defenses went right back up, and I told him that I simply couldn't provide him that information for security reasons. He started to contest and ask again, but Habib stepped in and explained that the US military doesn't share that information with people outside the military. He was right, of course, but I was surprised he knew how the US military worked and how quick he was to protect me from any more questions.

I began to wonder who this Habib guy really was and where he obtained his US military knowledge. The doctors had seen me limping in and wanted to provide whatever assistance they could. The orthopedic surgeon helped me over to a long couch, sat me down, and started asking questions regarding my leg. I told him I injured it on landing, and he started to gently feel around my knee and test the joint. I trusted him, as I had previously incurred a shoulder injury in high school that required surgery. The way he was holding my leg and knee, gently pushing and pulling to make sure the muscles, ligaments, and tendons were all okay, just felt like the touch of a doctor. After a quick examination, he said nothing was life threatening, but he wanted to get an X-ray. I was in pain but didn't figure there was an X-ray machine there and didn't want to continue to move around the city, so I thanked him and just asked for some ice.

While he went off to get the ice, the female doctor sat down and asked if I wanted anything for the pain, as she brought out a little packet. She said it was a painkiller, but I had never seen a painkiller that was in powder form from a packet about the size of a packet of ketchup. Not knowing what it was, and willing to push through the pain, I thanked her but said I would be fine.

As she was offering me painkillers, a man walked up with a (no kidding) gold platter, holding water, pop, and beer on it and offered me whatever I wanted. He presented it like a trained server would at a fancy hotel. At that point, I was having a pretty crappy day and would have liked nothing more than to drink a cold beer. I declined, knowing that as soon as I was in US hands, they would run blood tests, and I didn't want to have to answer why there was alcohol in my system. When I said I would just have water, (I knew it was the safer option), she looked at me and said, "You don't trust us, do you?"

It wasn't that I didn't trust them, but I was on guard, I wanted to be home, and I felt the most conservative option was the best option in my current situation. The doc came back with the ice shortly after getting the bottle of water. They left me alone to ice my leg for five to ten minutes. When they came back, they asked the same question that had been asked a couple of times tonight, "Now what?" They were willing to help but didn't know what they needed to do. I was grateful for the help, though I didn't know exactly what to do either.

Really, I just wanted to be on a plane, heading to safety in the hands of the US military. I checked the radio in hopes I had received a response to my earlier message. "On the way to Benghazi. Looking for some guidance." No such luck. I was still wary of using the radio voice function to call, based on the comm I received last time I used it in the presence of locals. I realized the radio was of no immediate use to me, but I still needed to reach someone who could get me on a plane out of Benghazi and hopefully Libya.

I knew a plane ride out was most likely not going to happen as part of our presence there was to support the no-fly zone. I figured the most likely way out was with the Navy, but I had no idea how to get in contact with them. I had asked Habib about the ability to call someone from RAF Lakenheath, and he told me that there was an issue with calls going outbound. Gaddafi had cut the cord on outbound international calls, but they could be received.

As I sat on the couch, I noticed the other doctor had an iPod touch. Having been living overseas, I used

Skype all the time to call my parents. I knew with the new iPods you could use the Skype app to call anyone in the world, you just needed an internet connection as they didn't have cellular data like an iPhone. I asked him if there was anywhere in the hotel that had Wi-Fi. He said there was an internet café on the second floor, but it was not very secure. I didn't really know exactly what he meant when he said "not secure" but knew I needed to let someone with more resources than I currently had know where I was.

They were looking to me to find my own way out and, with the radio not providing much help, I figured this was my best bet. We went up to the room that had internet. It turned out to be much more of a room and less of a café, but it had Wi-Fi. I asked if I could use his iPod to get in contact with the military. Thankfully, he happily obliged. I knew the number to the operations desk at RAF Lakenheath so that was my first call. It kept saying the call could not go through, even after trying it multiple times. The room was not secure, and I could tell my friends were not excited to be lingering, but I needed time to figure out the international calling issue. I called one of the few numbers I had memorized which might have someone on the other end who could help me. Even in 2009, most people had cellphones, and less and less did you really try to memorize someone's number because it was always in your phone. Without my phone, not being married, and with only my memory for the number, I dialed my parents. Thankfully, whatever mistake I was making trying to dial the UK was not an issue calling the US.

While the phone was ringing, I was not worried or nervous to talk to my parents. I was simply problem solving and trying to find a way out of Libya. This was not the first time I had called my parents when things were not going well. It had actually kind of become a thing. I would call them and tell them I was in the hospital, but I was okay and then tell them what happened and why I was there. Or the time I got hit by a car on my motorcycle—my sixth fight for life *(Calamity Six)*, I simply said, "I have been side-swiped by a car on the motorcycle. I am on the side of the road. I am fine, but my wrist might be a little messed up, and the cops are on the way." Get the bad news out first, followed shortly by everything is all right.

My dad answered the phone, and I told him, "I am alive and in Benghazi. I need you to call a number for me." By specifically saying, I was alive I was trying to convey this was not a normal "something bad has happened," but more of a "something really, really bad has happened." I gave them the number of the operations desk in England and told them to inform the military I was at a hotel in Benghazi. I guess ultimately hoping my parents would be the go between for my rescue.

As I was talking to my dad and giving him the number, "Cleopatra" had brought her laptop up, and it was on the Google homepage. I figured I might as well Google "international calling to the UK." I quickly realized my initial error calling back to the squadron. I hadn't been out of the UK enough to call back in and had forgotten the country code was +44 not +42. Now that I could call the OPS desk myself, I told my dad I would talk to him later and not to worry about calling the number I had given him; everything would be fine. *Not so fine for Mom!*

DORENE

It didn't take long for March 21, 2011, to roll in. It was Monday evening, and I was spending time caring for my elderly mother. Bruce called to say, "I received an interesting call from Tyler tonight. When I picked up the phone, the first thing I heard was, 'I am alive, and I'm okay. I am in Benghazi. I need you to get me the phone number of the base at Lakenheath.'" I said, "This is not good! Something has gone terribly wrong! I will be on my way home now." So, I left immediately and began to make the dash home. The pit in my stomach returned. It occured to me that this could be a code. This was Tyler's way of saying that something had gone very wrong, but he was alive.

I immediately called a friend in the military for advice. He confirmed my suspicions of an incident. However, he was not at liberty to share intel information. He recommended I email the base commander to inquire about Tyler's well-being. I never knew that was even an option. I called Bruce. "I am stopping by the church in hopes that someone will be there to let me in." I was compelled to sit with the chalice where our Lord is in the tabernacle.

Our church had a twenty-four-hour adoration. Certainly, someone would let me in. Well, in fact, someone was there. The lights were on, but the doors were locked.

I pounded furiously on the door, but to no avail. I just wanted to feel the presence of the Lord and give Tyler whatever fighting chance I could. Disappointed, I turned and ran for my car to head for home. As you might suspect, I did find the presence of the Lord—right there in my car! I was sure I could feel him riding shotgun! I was assured at that moment that everything was going as planned—though I still had no idea what the plan was. I would go home, sit with Bruce, and wait, hopeful, so hopeful, Tyler would call again, and we would hear his voice. I knew it was all I needed in order to determine his emotional state of being. It's that "sixth sense"—a mother's gift.

Now faith is confidence in what we hope for and assurance about what we do not see.

HEBREWS 11:1

Oddly enough, God continually brought this reminder into our lives at the most peculiar moments. The countless times we would look at the clock and see 11:1, or 1:11, 11:11, and we would glance at each other, knowing it was a reminder from Him to "keep the faith," even in the unknown!

Upon arriving at home, I immediately sat down at the computer, grabbed the mouse, and searched the web for information on how to contact the wing commander at Lakenheath. The email read, "We have reason to believe that Mask (Tyler's Air Force call sign) is in Benghazi and may be in harm's way. Can you tell us if he is OK?" The base wing commander later conveyed to us that when he received our email, he was quite taken by the fact that, "This is the first and only email I had received regarding this event, and it comes from the mother of Mask? How could this possibly be?" I assured him it must have been mother's intuition. (I felt the need to keep my resources "classified," as they say in the military.) I disclosed to him later that a military friend had given me the suggestion. May I just add he never responded to my email. He said he was so shocked by it, he didn't know how he would have responded, even if he was allowed to at the time.

YOUR SON IS WITH MY SON.
HE IS WITH THE SHEPHERD,
AND HE WILL BE KEPT SAFE.

chapter nine

THE SHEPHERD

---

*"But I will rescue you on that day,"
declares the LORD; "you will not be given into
the hands of those you fear. I will save you;
you will not fall by the sword but will escape
with your life, because you trust in me,
declares the LORD."*

JEREMIAH 39:17-18

The Second Phone Call

TYLER

Now that I had the country code figured out, I was optimistic when I called the 494th Operations Desk, hoping to hear one of the bros in the squadron answer and tell him what was going on. I knew had one heck of a story to share! But the phone just rang and rang . . . no one answered. The operations were being flown out of Aviano and so the desk at the squadron was not manned that time of day. What I should have done was call the command post through the base operator, but I didn't think of it at the time, and honestly, as a young guy, I didn't know they were the folks you should call, as they are always manned. I struck out on my Skype call to Lakenheath. I hadn't talked to anyone, and to my knowledge, no one was any closer to mounting a rescue to my location. I had to keep brainstorming. I needed another idea to orchestrate my own rescue.

Looking around, I noticed everyone was staring at me in the internet room, with puzzled faces over why this poor downed airman couldn't reach anyone but his parents. They waited for my next move. I took myself out of the role of a downed flyer and thought, *Who would I call if I was in a foreign country and needed government help to get out?* The State Department.

They help civilians get out of a country in chaos all the time due to rebellion or natural disaster, so I thought my situation would qualify. As I started Googling "US State Department," Habib said he *knew* someone from the US State Department. I figured this was too good to be true (coincidence?) and again was immediately suspect of his help. He got the number from his phone, and I called. I must have interrupted someone from after work drinks as the background was very loud.

I simply said my name, explained I was given his number from Habib, and I was a downed airman in Benghazi looking for some help. He told me to call him back on his office number in thirty minutes.

No one wanted to wait around that long in the non-secure internet café, so we went back downstairs. This would be the first of many trips up and down those stairs throughout the night as the elevator was out. Just my luck! The second floor was really the equivalent to the third floor as it was about twenty-five steps to get there. I know this because my knee was still in a lot of pain, and I was counting those steps going up and down. It was no easy task hobbling up the stairs and using controlled hops down the stairs—I grabbed both handrails and jumped from one step to another on my good leg. Once we got downstairs everyone was happy yet concerned whether this person from the State Department would actually be able to find me some help.

I didn't want to miss the call window, so our time back in the lobby was brief. Then it was back to hobbling up the stairs. When I finally got the gentleman from the State Department on the phone, I was happy to be talking to someone from the US government. However, I still could not 100 percent trust him and wanted to verify his identity and that he actually did work for the US government. I knew from training you could always give your name, rank, service number (SSN), and date of birth. There was no way for them to know my birthday as I still had my military ID, so I gave him my SSN and asked him to tell me my date of birth. When he told me the correct day, I was finally able to breathe easier. The connection was pretty bad due to poor internet connectivity, but he got my name, Benghazi, and the name of the hotel that we were at, the El Fadeel Hotel.

I had his phone number and knew he would be at that number should I call again, but the comms were not good via Skype, so Habib asked someone to find a satellite phone. Since the last communication was pretty limited, I had to call him back to give additional information on my status, who I was with, and the conditions in Benghazi. They were primarily concerned with the viability of coming to get me in Benghazi.

After another walk up to the internet room and failed attempt due to bad connection, Habib found someone with a satellite phone. Great! Because at this point, my knee couldn't take any more of those stairs! This presented a new problem. The satellite phone had to be used outside, with a clear line of sight to the sky. My hosts didn't like me being outside as it was not considered safe, even though we were in the heart of Benghazi. For them, the fight against Gaddafi was at its peak, and the people there were ready for a fight. After getting a good connection with the State Department, I was *finally* able to apprise them of my situation and let them know the condition I was in.

Once they had a better idea of my status, they began to formulate a plan and told me the next comm window would be in the next hour. The next call brought some good and unexpected news. They said they had a plan to get me picked up. My heart started to race, hoping it would be the fastest way possible, which was to bring a helicopter into Benghazi and take me to a Navy boat off the coast in the Mediterranean Sea. Their plan was not quite as direct as that or as convenient. They told me they had good success at the crash site, and that would be the location of my pickup. The "good success" they mentioned had to be MeSo Harney getting picked up, so he was safe, which was awesome news.

The problem was I didn't know where the crash site was. I didn't have time to take my coordinates, and the people I was now with didn't pick me up, so they didn't know either. As they conveyed their plan to me, I asked them to hold to see if Habib was willing and able to take me to the crash site. I was hoping he had heard where they found me and would be able to take me back, but he had no idea. Knowing the State Department could not give me exact coordinates of where they were going to pick me up on an unsecured line, I asked for general coordinates. They quickly passed them to me, and I told him I would call back in thirty minutes. It was time for another trip up to the internet room and some use of Google Maps on the iPod touch to figure out where we were actually going.

I wasn't crazy about the plan he passed onto me. Surely, the crash site had gathered a lot of attention at this point and the more people that were there the more potential risk existed for me, the recovery forces, and those who were trying to help. But it was a plan, and I wanted to get back to England. On our way to the internet room, Habib voiced similar concerns with the State Department's plan. His worry was the exposure to threats if we went outside of Benghazi and outside of the checkpoints. I plugged in the coordinates. When he saw where it was, he became even more concerned, as he realized just how far outside the city we were going to have to go. He said he didn't like the plan. I didn't either, but it was the only plan we had.

When I called the State Department thirty minutes later to get more information and let them know that Habib was willing to take me and we knew how to get there, they had come up with a new plan! Greater minds had prevailed, and they now wanted me to stay where I was, in the relatively safe hotel, and wait for pickup. I thought, just maybe, just hoping, it might be the express trip out of there on a helicopter, but that was not to be. They said the extraction wouldn't take place for another couple of hours, so to hang tight and they would call Habib's phone when they were close so I could come downstairs. I was then put on with an admiral and a general who both reassured me things would be fine. Before I hung up with the general, he said, "It should be over soon, and when it is, you will have one hell of a story to tell!" Feeling pretty positive about the new plan, I hung up and we went upstairs to a hotel room to wait for the next couple of hours.

All things considered, it was a very nice room in what was a war-torn city and country. The room had a king-size bed, large couch, chaise lounge, flat-screen TV and was opulently decorated. It also had a nice view of the Mediterranean Sea from the porch since it was on the fifth floor. I was there with a group of people, and when we got settled in the room, one of the gentlemen asked me if I wanted protection and offered me his AK-47. As cool as that would have been in some ways, I didn't want someone to take a picture of me with an AK-47 and post it online. It would send the wrong message.

Plus, I still had my 9mm Beretta pistol, so I politely refused. Habib started to tell me about what it was like in Benghazi and Libya with the current revolution happening and how it impacted his family. He told me he used to work at the embassy in Tripoli, which explained how he knew someone in the US State Department. As we sat and talked about families, both his and mine, he wanted to show me the atrocities that were happening in his country, so we turned on the news. There were graphic videos and images of rebels, women, and children who were gravely wounded and some dead. He was trying to convince me Gaddafi was a terrible person. He wanted my opinion on President Obama's reaction and involvement and to know how much support and in what form the President would be offering help to Libya.

Politics are a difficult conversation to have even with friends, so it put me in a difficult situation. Though this was not his intent, he was looking at me as the only US representative who he had seen face to face since the revolution started. However, I was not in a position to give any commitment level of the President or comment politically on the situation. I continued to acknowledge how terrible the situation was and confirmed we were providing air support, which was how I ended up in the situation I was in. How long and how much air support would continue was far above my pay grade. Once he realized I wasn't going to commit to anything politically, we changed the subject back to our families.

After a couple of hours, they began offering me tokens of my stay in Benghazi, signed money with their name, time, date, and place. The Egyptian doctors wanted a picture with "the American pilot"; I wasn't sure this was a great idea, but part of me did want something to look back on to remember. I still felt I could show nothing more than a neutral look, which was the reason I was not smiling in the photo.

Of course, Habib wanted one as well since we had been together the longest through this incredible journey. At around 06:00, right on time, Habib's phone rang. My ride was close, and we started to move downstairs. I said thank you over and over for the help everyone provided and encouraged them to stay as safe as they could. Much later, I found out how gravely my life was in danger and how much I owed my life to these men. Unbeknownst to me, before I had left the crash site, Gaddafi's forces had been only minutes behind me, according to an article that later reported:

Last Friday, regime troops were on the outskirts of Benghazi... Colonel Gaddafi vowed that his men would be going house to house, room to room, to burn out the opposition.

Crilly, Kirkup, & Winnett, 2011

They had truly saved me. (*Calamity Seven*)

Three Egyptian doctors assisted in initial medical care and communications.

Due to the confidential nature of my rescue by the US government, the details of the extraction method used to get me out of Benghazi will remain unsaid, but I did end up on an Italian frigate (warship) in the Mediterranean. When I got on board, I was greeted by several Italians who were obviously concerned with something, but I do not speak Italian, so I had no idea what they wanted. One of the officers came up and said I would have to surrender my pistol, as it was not allowed for anyone but the military police or rescue forces to carry weapons aboard the boat, but he would give it back before I left.

At this point, it didn't matter; I was in friendly hands, so I gladly gave him my pistol. I had been awake thirty hours and was dog-tired. They showed me to my room, which I was pretty sure was not a free bunk but one that had been given up for my use. Although my knee was still in a lot of pain and I was limping around, the cabin was on the third level below the deck. Navy ships from any country are not known for their wide ladders (stair-ways) or corridors, and it was a challenge to get below decks to my room. Once there, I was finally left alone to get a shower and rest. I was still in a little bit of survival mode when I got on the ship. It was not until I got in the shower that I could feel my body finally start to relax, and the events of the past thirty hours started to catch up to me. I passed out on the bunk before my head hit the pillow.

DORENE

Back in Colorado, with nothing to do now, but wait . . . again. Night fell, sleep came, and the phone rang at approximately 4:30 a.m. "This is the 494th Commander with the United States Air Force." We all know that Air Force personnel do not just call to check in or chat. They contact family only when operations have failed. My heart stopped temporarily, my eyes opened wide, my foggy brain looked for some clarity to sort through it all, and I realized this isn't a dream! "I am calling to tell you there has been an incident involving your son, Mask. We will continue to use his call sign, to protect his identity. Before I go any further, we need to have your word, you will not breath a word of this to anyone. Not family, not friends, not employers—no one. If this is not possible, we cannot continue with this conversation, as it will compromise the safe return of your son to England."

Of course, we agreed to any and all conditions required to obtain information! Fortunately, we did not have to turn over any other family members as part of the negotiations. It was important for us to realize, per his request, that if any of this information was to get out in an email, text, social media, etc., it could easily compromise the safe return of Mask and MeSo. We completely understood the importance of this.

"What time is it there?" he inquired. "Have you been watching the news?" I thought to myself, *Of course not! You just woke me from a sound sleep!*

"You should turn your station to CNN. When they show the news story of a downed F-15E Strike Eagle over Benghazi, you will know this is Mask and MeSo's plane. We have information they both ejected, and we believe they have been separated and are still alive. We have very little information at this time on Mask's whereabouts. We will do our best to communicate with you every six to twelve hours or as we are able. In the meantime, continue to watch the news, as you will have an updated awareness on the story."

We immediately turned on the TV, and propped ourselves up in bed, with eyes wide open, to watch the story unfold. Immobilized, we saw a crashed, badly burned and mostly destroyed F-15E. There were many locals walking around it, on top of it, searching through the debris in bewildered curiosity.

After the shock and awe of what we just observed, slightly subsided, I looked at Bruce and said, "Does this feel familiar to you in an eerie sort of way? Are you feeling the same thing I am? Are you reliving the same emotions now, as you did while helplessly watching Columbine unfold? Knowing there has been a tragedy that involved your child, yet not knowing where he was."

He gazed back at me with an expression that needed no words. We were reliving the same memory that still lived deep in our hearts. At least this time, unlike Columbine, we knew he was alive! However, that's about all we knew!

We took shifts going to the bathroom, so we wouldn't miss a word or moment of new information, while waiting for six o'clock to notify our friends, Mike and Paula. We knew they would be up and around about then, and we didn't want to alarm them with an early morning wake-up call. They disclosed they had already been up and were watching the report on the news so they were not completely alarmed by our phone call. Here is yet another example of God taking care of the small details.

Keep in mind, this was Tuesday, March 21, 2011, and we were scheduled to leave the following Friday on our previously arranged vacation to England. While waiting to update Mike and Paula on our current events, we realized we needed to decide on our trip. Should we go anyway, or should we follow the advice from Tyler and the commander to wait? The squadron commander had made it clear; he had not spoken with Mask yet and had no idea of his whereabouts or when or how he would be returned to Lakenheath. We decided to hold off on that decision until we could communicate with the commander again.

Avoiding sharing information with anyone became an interesting challenge. We were to carry on as normal. Really? Bruce and I both knew we needed to be home to digest and process what had and still was transpiring. We both called into work sick, using my "sickly" mother as our crutch. We thought our subterfuge would be successful; however, there were a number of people who were pretty aware, and they were able to put some things together after watching the news.

"So, Dorene, surely you know about the F-15E that crashed! They aren't giving names of the pilots, and you weren't at work yesterday. I have a creepy feeling that this is Tyler." I could only respond with, "Yes, I did see that crash, but my mother has been quite ill." Fortunately, we had only one day left before our departure, so I had to work on my Academy Award performance for only those two days!

Later that evening, the call came. Tyler's commander called and shared with us that Tyler had requested he contact us, so we could postpone our trip to Lakenheath.

Tyler's location had now been identified, and we were informed he had been rescued by the local rebels. He was now in the care of the US military. God bless those rebels! His return arrival could easily take a week or two, depending on the debriefing, logistics, investigations, and the mental state of *both* airmen. No man would be left behind. They would come home *together*, even though they had been separated during the ejection. We now knew we had Tyler in Benghazi and the four of us in the States. Nothing was certain. We had only two days to decide if we should wait until he returned to Lakenheath, or if we should just go. What would you do? Could God really make this happen in just a few days? The military said, "No way!"

We responded, "Yes, we understand your recommendation is to stay home. However, we gave this to God before Tyler left on his deployment, and God has prearranged our dates to His divine design. So, we shall take the step of faith and carry on with our trip as planned." Internally, we knew we would not be leaving Lakenheath until we were reunited with Tyler. God had a plan! How gracious He was to continue encouraging us to keep our faith through the repeated appearances of 11:1.

We shared the information and our thoughts with Mike and Paula, and they decided they would be on board and come along.

It was time to put out another email to the family.

Date: Wednesday, March 23, 2011, 7:41 PM

Hello again,

So, we certainly have many reasons to thank you for your blanket of protection. Who was to know what was ahead and why we were asking you for prayer? Up until this time, we have been unable to share what has been going on in our lives these past few days.

Many of you may have seen on the news that there was an F-15E Strike Eagle that went down over Benghazi due to mechanical difficulties last Tues. This was Tyler's plane. He has been rescued and is back with the US military.

In fact, if any of you would like to read a few brief articles about the ordeal, the best place we have found so far is to Google "Telegraph, UK."

You have, once again, been there for us in thoughts and prayers (we enjoy returning the favor) and making a difference in the outcome of a life. We believe, without a doubt, your prayers were instrumental in this entire event.

"Thank you" hardly touches our gratitude for the outcome of this story. Our continued prayer is that total healing of mind, body, and spirit will complete the story. At least this chapter—as I believe, it has just begun. . . .

In the meantime, his squadron commander was keeping in touch now and then but had very limited knowledge as far as any updates he could share regarding Tyler's location or well-being. All we really knew, which was the most important, was that he was in safe hands. There was also an indication he had injured his leg, but there was no information as to what extent. All that mattered to us was that our son was *alive* and *safe*.

At this point, the lieutenant colonel expressed his admiration for the calmness and faith we had displayed up until then. He shared this in our next phone conversation. "I have never seen a family with the ability to remain so calm . . . unlike any other. I find that same demeanor to be true with Mask as well. He also displayed amazing peace and calm throughout his landing and rescue. There is something quite different and special about your family. I am looking forward to meeting the parents of this fine young man."

We were very humbled by his comment and assured him that it was indeed divine design working in our lives. He replied, "Yes, I am a believer, too. I read the Bible every day, but I don't have what you have. It is something special."

And the peace of God, which passeth all understanding, shall keep your hearts and minds through Christ Jesus.

PHILIPPIANS 4:7

It truly is the experience of peace beyond all understanding. We did not even understand it. We just knew we had it and where it came from.

He also informed us to go online and look up *The Telegraph*. He explained the paper would be posting updated information faster than he could call us, with time change and military restrictions on public information. *The Telegraph* would not have the same restrictions as the Air Force. That was exactly what we did. What a valuable piece of information that was! Here is the story that was posted the next day:

(As you are reading this article, take special care to note the symbolism God provided to us. I was reading this in the morning, just out of bed, eyes barely open, with no time for my first cup of coffee. The story of a "Shepherd," if you will, who came out to find the lost sheep.)

US JET CRASHES IN LIBYA: AIRMAN WOULD NOT HAVE KNOWN WHETHER HE FACED FRIEND OR FOE.

The US airman would not have known whether the armed men advancing towards him were friendly Rebels or soldiers loyal to Colonel Gaddafi.

© Rob Crilly / Telegraph Media Group Limited 2011

12:07PM GMT 22 Mar 2011

Behind him his F15 Strike Eagle was a burning wreck.

He (Mask) had parachuted into a field of sheep somewhere near Benghazi airbase and needed to escape – his fellow crew member had landed in another field nearby.

Raising his hands in the air he called out "OK, OK" to greet the crowd. But he need not have worried. "I hugged him and said don't be scared we are your friends," said Younis Amruni, 27.

The airman was one of dozens taking to the air to patrol a no-fly zone over Libya and take out Colonel Gaddafi's air defenses. They have turned the tide in the desert war, helping Rebels keep the government from attacking their stronghold in Benghazi, about 45-minute drive away.

A queue formed to shake the hand of the airman, as locals thanked him for his role in the attacks. Witnesses said it was around midnight when they heard two planes streak out of the Libyan sky.

Mohamed Breek came out of his home a couple of hundred yards away to see what was happening above his flower-studded meadow where his sheep were grazing.

"It was on fire," he said. "We didn't hear any shots it just fell from the sky by itself and then there was a big explosion." A rescue helicopter swooped low to collect the second crew member (Meso) – and strafed the ground to keep the locals at bay. Bullets tore through Mr. Amruni's driveway and gate.

"We are so grateful to these men who are protecting the skies," he said. "We gave him juice and then the revolutionary military people took him away."

On Tuesday morning, the blackened wreckage was still smoldering. A guided missile lay at its side. The wings had been ripped from the long-range bomber and its two tail fins stood high above the grass, attracting opposition supporters and souvenir hunters alike.

Plane crashed and burned.
© Sebastian Meyer/Telegraph Media Group Limited 2023

Last Friday, regime troops were on the outskirts of Benghazi... Colonel Gaddafi vowed that his men would be going house to house, room to room, to burn out the opposition. Libyan troops were reportedly committing atrocities in outlying areas of the city.

TYLER'S SEVEN CALAMITIES

From six calamities He will rescue you;
in seven no harm will touch you. (Job 5:19)

1. Birth
2. Blood
3. Spin/Ejection
4. Columbine
5. The Hunt
6. Motorcycle Accident
7. Rescued

For this is what the Sovereign LORD says:
"I myself will search for my sheep and look
after them. As a shepherd looks after his scattered
flock when he is with them, so will I look after
my sheep. I will rescue them from all the places
where they were scattered on a day of clouds
and darkness. I will bring them out from
the nations and gather them from the countries,
and I will bring them into their own land."

EZEKIEL 34:11-13

What do you think? If a man owns a hundred sheep,
and one of them wanders away, will he not leave the
ninety-nine on the hills and go to look for the one that
wandered off? And if he finds it, truly I tell you,
he is happier about that one sheep than about the
ninety-nine that did not wander off. In the same
way your Father in heaven is not willing that
any of these little ones should perish.

MATTHEW 18:12-16

While these verses relate to our spiritual existence and relationship with God, the symbolism for me was God's way of letting me know of His protection around Tyler in one of the sweetest ways He could have done so.

It brought joyous tears as I felt God touch my heart. "Are you kidding me, Lord? Of all the places you find to ground him—a field with sheep? Found by a shepherd? Does it get any better than this?"

He responded with that gentle voice once again. *Your son is with my son. He is with the Shepherd, and he will be kept safe.* There was a long pause as He waited for me to try to compose myself in the midst of emotions I cannot describe. And then the voice comes again: *He is alive because you believed in Me. He lives because you were obedient in your faith. In you, daughter, I am well pleased.*

At this point, you can only imagine I was brought to my knees, literally feeling God holding me. My body could not physically hold the energy I felt around me. Our language has no words to capture that intimate moment. It was a moment that took me quite some time to be able to share with people and remain composed while speaking. The tears still stream down my face as I write.

The news of Tyler's rescue was another confirmation that God's divine design was in full motion, and we were to carry on with our plans to fly to England, By now, I was exuding gratitude for the kind and gentle way He had powerfully confirmed His plans for us.

Keep in mind, we were still not able to share anything in regard to this with family, friends, or strangers, for that matter!

In Tyler's recollection of his ejection, you have read about exactly what measures God took to remove Tyler's

What are the odds, that we should happen upon a statue like this in London?

The Good Shepherd *by Sharon Collins.*

control of the situation. Things looked like coincidences or human error, but in fact, it was the perfect plan.

Tyler asked me once, "How could all of that have been so perfect? How did I not feel any fear when the circumstances—and training—said I should? I don't recall even praying."

"Oh," I replied with laughter, "you didn't need to! The rest of us did that!"

The blanket of protection, the power of prayer—therein lies the glory of God's story.

As we discussed our plans with Trevor, he expressed a longing in his heart to go with us. He, too, wanted to be there to welcome his brother home to Lakenheath, but it seemed quite the challenge to even entertain the idea. It was the work of God that allowed Trevor to come—go figure! He had just started a new job as a leadership trainer with classes and commitments he was obligated to and no vacation or personal time. His supervisor advised he should not go. Trevor told us he would just take the consequences. Whether it cost him his job or not, his brother's life was far more important than the lack of understanding from this supervisor, and God would work it out. We'd just leave it with Him.

Next, we tried to obtain tickets at the last minute, which would probably come at a fairly high price. We had only about forty-eight hours before departing, and our flight was completely booked. In addition, the lieutenant colonel had arranged to have us picked up at the airport by Air Force personnel who would bring us to the base. So logistically, Trevor's flight times would need to align with ours to keep things running smoothly. What are the chances? Typically, with international travel, chances are not likely. With God in the details, anything is possible!

We decided the best thing to do would be, once again, to give it to God. If it was His desire to have the family there, it would certainly work out. In the grand scheme of things, this would be easy for God. So, it won't surprise you to know that Trevor did indeed find a ticket on a different flight that would land in England within thirty minutes of ours! Wondering about the price? Trevor paid half the ticket price of ours, which we had booked four months prior! Bonus!

The next call we received from Tyler's commander was on Thursday. This was the day just prior to our leaving. He had a surprise for us. "Mask is on the other end of the phone!" Our conversation was limited to ten minutes and would be monitored, but oh, what joy in our hearts to finally hear the voice of "the lost sheep"! Perhaps you could liken it to the feelings of the Shepherd upon hearing the sound of the lost sheep he was seeking.

Tyler informed us during the conversation it could take at the very least, three to seven days before he arrived in Lakenheath (most likely the seven days) and tried to discourage us from coming until there was a confirmed date. We assured him God would figure it out. It was not a concern for us, but more importantly, we did not want it to be a concern for him. His focus needed to be elsewhere. He then expressed how much he longed to see his brother as well, but he knew Trevor's situation and understood if it would not be feasible. In keeping with our surprise, we assured him his brother would want to be there, but simply couldn't make the trip, although we would bring his love with us to share. It never has the same impact as it does in person. Though one could hear the disappointment in his voice, Mask kept his brave heart steady and accepted it. There is just something healing and warm having family around in the midst of a crisis. Oh, wasn't he in for a surprise!

Though time was running low on preparations for Friday's departure, I was compelled to find something for Tyler that would be symbolic of this event. I literally had about one hour to spare to run around for this project. So, once again, relying on God to lend His assistance, I inquired as to what it could be – while also reminding Him it would need to fit in my suitcase! The thought immediately came to me that it should include the shepherd and the sheep. "Perfect," I thought. "What a great idea, Lord!" The next question, of course, was: "Where should I begin to look?" Well, there were two religious stores close, so in asking for guidance, I ended up at Mardel, a Christian store.

As I was running across the parking lot, I was talking to God. "Okay, so we don't have much time. I am just going to run in and ask the first person I see for what I am looking for." Great! We have a plan! I ran through the entrance to find a salesclerk literally standing at the door as if she was waiting just for me!

"May I help you?"

"Yes, I am looking for something that would symbolize the shepherd and the sheep. It can be anything that will fit in a suitcase. Perhaps a necklace, a book, a figurine, a picture, anything. What is the first thing that comes to your mind?"

"Well, it's funny you should ask," she replied. "We just finished unpacking a load of pictures in the back of the store. I believe there is a picture of a shepherd."

I immediately thought: *A picture, a frame. Will I have room? Oh well, I must look. This was the plan.*

Ah, yes, indeed. There it was—the perfect picture! Christ, the shepherd, stood next to a sheep in a field! Yes, that's right! Perfect! A 10" x 12" wrapped canvas print with no frame! Perfect for my suitcase! I was overjoyed with the find. It was such a bonus. Nothing I had to have, but just something my heart had desired in the midst of the storm. Not at all a complement to Tyler's décor, but nonetheless, it was a symbolic memory of his ejection and capture.

So, I had shopped, purchased, returned home, and wrapped that beautiful piece of art in one hour. I know it sounds like, "Yeah, right," but it is the truth. Time was of the highest priority.

In the meantime, we continued our communication with the Air Force personnel, regarding logistics for travel, lodging, etc.

chapter 10

HEADING TO LAKENHEATH

"For I know the plans and thoughts that I have for you," says the LORD, "plans for peace and well-being and not for disaster, to give you a future and a hope."

JEREMIAH 29:11 AMP

TYLER

When I woke up, I didn't really know where I was or for how long I had been asleep. It was around 6:30 in the evening of the same day, and I was starving. I made my way to the officer's mess, where the crew was just finishing up dinner. The ship's captain saw me and offered me food. I quickly accepted and the kitchen crew stopped cleaning up to make me a fresh plate of delicious pasta. While it was being prepared, the captain offered me his stateroom, which had a computer and internet access. The first thing

I did was log into my email and send a message to my parents and Kelly that I was all right. No details, just that I was okay. Next order of business was to Google "F-15E crash in Libya" and see what was on the web about our jet. I saw, for the first time, the pictures of the crash and the burned-out carcass of our jet; it was sobering.

What I didn't know at the time was that Kelly had received the email, already fearing it was me. My email was confirmation to her (even though I never confirmed it in the email) that it was me and my jet. Only minutes after she got the email, my roommate and squadron mate, Clint, called Kelly. He had known it was me as soon as the jet went down, but it is normal for the Air Force to wait to notify family and make the information public until the service member is either in safe hands or confirmed as a POW or KIA. My email beat the official news by five minutes. When Clint told Kelly it was my jet and I was okay, she replied, "Yeah, I know. I just got an email from him. Obviously, Clint was a little surprised I was emailing people and that she already had heard from me. With notifications done, I went to eat dinner. As is customary in Italy, you have wine with dinner and maybe an after-dinner drink, like Jägermeister, to aide digestion. I was still worried that in the near future, I was going to get the full work up from the medical folks and turned down any alcohol, even though it would have hit the spot.

We had to wait for several hours for the Huey helicopter to return to take me to the Italian aircraft carrier. As I waited for its arrival in the cargo bay that opened up to the helicopter pad on the back of the ship, the surrealism of everything started to kick in. I was truly lucky to be out of Libya. Before hopping into the helicopter (helo), I made sure to give my thanks to the Italian captain and his crew for their hospitality. When the helicopter showed up, it took them a good twenty-five minutes to land as the seas were rough, and it was very windy. Not to mention, the landing pad was only slightly bigger than the helicopter itself. I was a little nervous knowing I would have to hop in next. Once the helo landed and refueled, one of the Italian enlisted security guys gave me back my pistol. I had kind of forgotten about it and really didn't care much at the moment. We then hopped on the helo and went to the Italian carrier.

After just experiencing a plane malfunction and ejecting less than forty-eight hours prior, I was not necessarily looking forward to riding in a low-altitude helicopter, seventy-five feet above the water, at night. It was a forty-minute or so ride and I was genuinely worried about crashing in this aircraft as well. I guess my trust in them was a little weak at that moment. Not to mention, it brought me back to 2006 when, during training with the US Navy, we had to get submerged in a mock helo with blackout goggles on and find our way out. It was very disorientating, and something I never wanted to have to do again.

The ride and landing on the deck of the much larger Italian aircraft carrier was uneventful. I was quickly whisked from the Huey to a much larger helicopter with a handful of other people looking to get back to the mainland. It was a clear night. I had the row to myself since it sat about eighteen people, and there were only five on board. Again, I had several minutes to appreciate how surreal my situation was. When we landed at Catania, Italy, I was briskly taken to a learjet that was already running, which quickly took off on its way to Rome. It must have been the only jet available that time of night because it felt like a private jet. It had a stewardess and very ornate décor with gold inlay armrests, and I had a nice, hot Italian meal from Southern Italy to Rome. When we landed in Rome, I was met by two air attachés, which were in charge of handing me off to official military personnel.

As we drove away from the airport, I recognized several Italian historical sites I had seen growing up and others I one day hoped to see: the Colosseum, a glimpse of the Pantheon, and the military headquarters at Piazza Venezia. I was able to see these sights only because it was about four in the morning and the City Centre was deserted on a weeknight. I had no idea where we were going, but one thing was certain, after waiting for the Huey from the frigate and stepping off one aircraft straight onto another over several hours, I really had to relieve my bladder!

I asked the major if there was anywhere we could stop, not really knowing much about Italy, which if I did, I would have known they don't really have public bathrooms in the middle of the night like the US does at gas stations. He offered to take me to his apartment. When we stopped on the street and started to walk away from the car, he realized I still had my gun on me. It is against the law for anyone besides the police to carry a gun in the city of Rome. I hid it under the seat and went upstairs to his extremely nice apartment.

It had to be, because part of being an Air Force attaché is having dinner parties and inviting guests, including important ones, to your house. I knew at that moment what I wanted to be later in life in the Air Force. This was the job for me! When I was done, we quickly returned to the car and headed for the south of Rome. We stopped at the front of a hotel where there were two guys waiting on the corner. They were clearly American and dressed in naval uniforms. I think one was an attaché and one was active duty in Naples, the closest US military base to Rome. I hopped in the car, and we started the two-and-a-half-hour drive to Naples. As soon as we started moving—I knew these guys, at least one of them was active-duty military—I felt safe and passed out. The two-and-a-half-hour trip for me felt like five minutes. I awoke as we approached the ever-familiar and much-appreciated sight of the gate guards to NAS (Naval Air Station) Naples.

Once there, I was escorted to the gym, where the locker room was cleared out, and was shown the way to the showers. The personnel recovery specialist who met me there had purchased from the base exchange some civilian clothes I could change into. That shower felt amazing, especially being on a US military base. Things began to feel normal again. Once cleaned up, the specialist laid out what I could expect as I made my way to Rota, Spain, for reintegration. My initial flight a couple of hours later was from Naples to Sigonella Air Base in Italy. We were there only to refuel and pick up the SERE psychologist who would complete Phase I of my reintegration on our way from Sigonella to Rota.

As we were taking off, the psychologist pointed out the city of Catania just out the window, saying he was stationed there a couple of assignments ago. To his surprise, I told him how ten hours prior, I had flown in there on my way to Naples. I could see he was a little confused on exactly what route I had taken to actually get where I was now. I was essentially looping back on myself, but I should save the explanation for the actual debrief. He was primarily concerned with my psychological well-being and any immediate concerns regarding the people who picked me up in Libya. Throughout the questioning, he asked me if I had ever been in any other stressful situations in my life. When I told him that I was a student at Columbine in the cafeteria during the shootings, he could only muster through his astonishment to reply, "That's an interesting data point." Surely nothing he had expected.

Once we arrived at NAS Rota, Spain, I was taken to the hospital for an exam. I had always heard that you get a very thorough exam if you eject but didn't know exactly what that meant. I found out later that it is common to do a full-body x-ray; that was definitely not what happened to me. It felt more like a routine doctor visit. I told him my knee hurt a fair amount but that I could walk, albeit with a limp. He gave me some weak painkillers and told me to stay off of it, but that was about it. I was expecting more of the third degree since we had lost a jet—urine sample, blood samples, the whole nine yards. What I didn't know until later was, at that point, they were calling it a combat loss, which meant there was no investigation into the mishap since it was during combat. In actuality, there was an investigation because we did not go down due to being shot down but for an unknown reason.

They took me to my hospital room, which had two beds and a small, attached room with a little table and a couple of chairs. Two young seamen were at the door to the room "as protection," though I wasn't sure who sent them. They wheeled in a small cart with books, whose genres ranged from children's books to romantic novels to other fiction. They also informed me that MeSo might be there later that night or the next morning. Then, the debriefings would begin. After being brought food and water, I was left by myself for the next eight hours. They had disabled the TVs, and there was no computer in the room—all to keep our memory of the incident pure and untainted by news coverage—so I was on my own with some books.

Not quite the welcome home I had expected, but it was good enough for me since I was alive and still in a little bit of survival mode. I selected a book I had read before, *The Lost World*, and started reading. It was nice to get my mind off the last couple of days, as up to that point it was like a video in my mind that would not stop playing, rewinding, playing, rewinding. The book at least took me away for a little bit.

The Lost World kept me occupied for the eight hours it took MeSo to get close enough on the amphibious assault ship USS *Kearsarge* to take a helicopter to Rota, Spain. When he walked in the door, I was really happy to see him, though part of me wanted to punch him for trying to kill me twice. Overwhelmingly, though, I was glad to see him again. After we hugged and said "hello," the staff told us the debriefings would start the following morning and that we weren't supposed to talk with each other about anything that happened so as not to influence our memories.

Of course, as soon as they left the room, we both looked at each other and said the same thing at the same time, "What the hell happened?" After discussing different theories of how we entered the spin such as, our bomb impacting our aircraft due to it not releasing properly, to getting hit by a missile, we spitballed ideas for an hour or so and then went to bed as we were both exhausted. When we woke up the next morning, we had a couple of hours before the debriefings were to begin, so we decided to find out where we went down in relation to Benghazi using the survival maps we flew with. Even under no pressure, no threats in the area, and plenty of light in a hospital room, it took us both twenty minutes to find out roughly where we went down. It didn't help that the maps we had were for the entirety of Libya, about one-fifth the size of the whole US.

At 10:00, MeSo was called in for the first round of debriefings. He was in there for about one and a half hours. When he was finished, lunchtime was spent discussing "what was it like for you?" until it was my turn after lunch. The debriefings took place in the hospital room next to ours. When I walked in, there were a couple of Intelligence folks, a SERE psychologist, a SERE specialist, an aviator from the base, a normal psychologist, a representative of the base leadership, and a representative from the office of nonconventional personnel recovery. Before I began, the rep told me to tell my story from the beginning and he would stop me at the part I was not allowed to talk about.

I went through my story and got to the same spot that I am sharing with you now, where again I will need to stop. He cleared everyone out of the room and turned on a white noise generator, and I told him about my journey from the hotel in Benghazi to the Italian frigate. He listened without really asking any questions. At the end he simply said, "That's all great. You will never talk about that, ever again."

He brought everyone back in, and I continued the rest of my story. After a couple of hours, we were done with the initial round and went back to our hospital room. We got a surprise around dinnertime when several guys, including my good buddy and roommate, as well as the squadron commander, showed up to welcome us back, in a manner of speaking. It was an amazing feeling to see the bros again, but they had been there less than a minute before they started giving us a hard time about crashing a jet. We expected nothing less.

Over the next couple of days, it was the same routine: MeSo in the morning and me in the afternoon with the bros bringing us dinner at night. There were some limitations they imposed on us as far as contact with family. On the second night, we were allowed to call family, supervised by the SERE specialist, to let them know how we were doing. We finally completed the debriefings and hopped on a plane with the bros. We had an entire C-130, capable of carrying ninety-four troops, all to ourselves, all six of us: me, MeSo, and four other military personnel sent from our base in Lakenheath.

DORENE

I was so excited! It was finally Friday, so we loaded up and drove to the airport. Our minds were spinning and miles away, already across the ocean. To focus on anything other than holding our son in our arms was really a stretch! After all, he was alive! And we were praising God with every breath.

We were almost out the door when the phone rang. It was Tyler! We have a quick ten-minute, monitored phone call with him. Just long enough for him to inform us there was no way he would be in the UK before Monday. Later in the week was most likely. He also expressed, yet again, his desire to have Trevor there with him. We kept our surprise (which was not at all easy) and acted disappointed that he could not come with us. The conversation ended, and we headed for the door when the phone rang again. "Hello?" Bruce answered. "Well, hello," said a woman on the other end of the line. Bruce anxiously explained that we were on our way out the door but asked, "May I help you?" "Yes," she said. "I am sorry to bother you. This is Ken Harney's mother."

We had never been told the pilot's name, so we had no point of reference until she explained. "I am the mother of the pilot who was flying with Mask. My son's call sign is MeSo." It was another one of those moments that stopped us in our tracks! She was curious to know if we were going to the UK and expressed her sadness that neither she, nor her husband, would be able to join up with everyone. My heart went out to her as a mother, knowing the desire we instinctively have to be with our children in times of trauma or crisis. We acknowledged her kindness in reaching out and assured her we would give her son a welcome home hug for her as well. Once again, we made tracks to the door as our friends Mike and Paula were awaiting their ride.

Knowing someone from the Air Force would be meeting us upon our arrival at Heathrow Airport, we had set a plan in place with Trevor. Since he was due to arrive in London thirty minutes prior to us, he would meet us at baggage claim. The agreement was no matter what happened, we would wait for him there. Mind you, we knew our cell phones would not work in London, so communication would be not only limited, but nonexistent. He arrived one hour before us, which turned out to be another real blessing.

You see, none of us knew there were two separate baggage claim areas that were a thirty-minute train ride apart! Poor Trevor! Upon learning he was at least thirty minutes from us, he began to fervently pray: "God, please don't let them leave. I will never be able to find them in this place. Please don't let them leave, please don't let them leave." (Remember, we were unable to use our cell phones, so a phone call was out of the question.) If you have ever had the chance to fly into Heathrow Airport and witness the chaos, you would certainly understand his concerns.

In the meantime, we were waiting downstairs in baggage claim, while the Air Force driver was waiting for us upstairs. It took the four of us quite some time to realize that no one could get to our baggage claim without a ticket to pass through security. This was a bit different from what we were used to in the States. We decided that, to make sure we didn't miss Trevor, we should get right outside of baggage claim. He had already realized he could not enter baggage claim, so he just kept praying for God's help in this unfamiliar airport.

As we come up the stairs, we spotted the Air Force personnel, which gave us some relief. We informed them we were short a family member, so we needed to wait awhile. They explained that there were multiple baggage claim areas. So, after waiting for a time, we decided we should locate an airport assistant and have Trevor paged.

As we turned and took a couple of steps, our traveling companion, Mike, calmly said, "Well, hello, Trevor." Mike was the only one who hadn't turned to leave. If not for him, we would have missed Trevor arriving by escalator at that moment. *Thank you, God, once again, for taking care of the details.* Finally, we could all relax, and Trevor's face, in particular, reflected his sense of relief. Airport missions accomplished!

The Air Force diplomats (who treated us like royalty and made us feel so welcome) now had our entire group. After loading up in the van, we all sighed with relief, with a sense of calm that we had actually arrived, were together, and on our way to Lakenheath Air Force Base. Though we enjoyed pleasant conversation and had some good laughs during the ride, we all knew that many unknowns still remained ahead of us. Our journey with God would continue to unfold.

Upon our arrival at Lakenheath AFB, we were shown around the base and brought to our accommodations. Our guide opened the door to our suite, and to our amazement, the counters and refrigerator were full of food, and a beautiful bouquet of flowers adorned the table. Their thoughtfulness brought tears. In addition, just to show their great sense of humor in the midst of a stressful time, they left a bottle of wine for Tyler. The label read,

"Bail Out!" Perfect! That broke the ice and gave us a good laugh. You can be sure Tyler has kept that bottle of wine!

By this time, we were all weary, having spent the past twenty-four hours traveling. Our Air Force guide suggested this would be a great time for a short nap, though he warned us that napping too long would really make a mess of our sleep/wake cycle. He said he would keep us informed if he heard any news. He also reiterated the last information he received was Tyler's estimated arrival time would be an additional three days. He further explained those three days could easily be extended. After the debriefings, assuming their mental states were stable enough, Mask and MeSo would return together. If one was ready, but the other was not, both would stay. No man was left behind.

Our family outside the base building.

We were fine with that. We had reserved a rental car and were sure we could find many things to do and see for three days. We all crashed out for about an hour and then discussed how we were going to get our rental car, since it was reserved in Cambridge, about an hour from the Air Force base. You see, Tyler was originally (three months prior to our visit) going to pick us up at the airport and bring us to Cambridge, where he resided. We would pick up the car and begin our tour of London, Bath, etc., while we waited for the men to return home. Those plans were obviously going to get scrapped.

However, shortly after waking from our brief rest, the commander called with an update. "We just received word there has been a schedule change! Mask and MeSo have now departed! They will be arriving in three hours rather than three days!" From a minimum of three days initially to now only three hours, how does that happen? This would be the last of thirteen legs Tyler had traveled to get home. They even rerouted a C-130 cargo plane to ensure they got home as soon as possible.

Upon these words, my body was filled with the Spirit of God. Once again, I felt His hand upon my shoulder. Another WOW moment as I looked at the big picture and the many details God took care of to bring all of us from the United States, and Tyler and MeSo from Benghazi with all the military red tape and security logistics in three days. Really? This was incomprehensible. Even the Air Force personnel were in disbelief. It was only by Divine Design! Upon hearing this message, my heart was completely filled with gratitude for the wonderful works He had done.

Have you ever heard the saying, "The devil is in the details"? He is, if you open the door of your mind and heart to that idea. Now you have given the devil permission to have that power in your life. That could be scary! How about a new perspective? God is in the details. Who has the power now?

At this point, it was suggested we might want to grab a bite to eat while we waited for an update. We invited our military guide, Lt. Col. Dano, and his wife to join us. As we enjoyed a lovely dinner with the two of them, he received a call asking if we would like to go out to the tarmac and meet Tyler and MeSo when they arrived. Well, you can imagine our delight in being asked to participate in that event! Who would say, "No thanks"?

The Air Force arranged for a van to pick us all up and drove us out to the tarmac, where we anxiously awaited the arrival of that C-130J. Estimated time of arrival was approximately 9:00 p.m. They had set up a military-media staging area, ready and waiting with cameras and huge lights.

We stepped out onto the tarmac and watched the plane land and begin its approach to the staging area. Then, and only then, did it really hit me. I was completely overwhelmed with the reality of what my eyes beheld. The power of that big metal bird symbolized the power of our military, its honor, its strength, and its fragile hearts. It also carried the pain of sacrifices given

On the bus from the base to the tarmac with Mike, Trevor, and Paula.

Waiting in the biting wind for our moment of reunion.

On the tarmac with military brass waiting for the arrival of Mask and MeSo.

over so many years. Inside, it also held the safe return of Mask and MeSo, who were now on "home" soil. It all came flooding in on me!

I wanted the plane to approach slowly so I could absorb the vastness of what God had just put before me. His kept promises, His divine intervention, His faithfulness in every detail. A downed and burning plane, ejection over enemy territory, a capture, a rescue, debriefings, emotional de-escalations, and thirteen moves through numerous countries in three days. Now, here we were together! The oceans and lands could not keep us apart. Was this really happening to all of us here? It was one of those "pinch me" moments. I felt like I was watching this happen to someone else.

I was completely consumed by His embrace, His peace, which really does pass beyond our understanding. There truly are no words to describe the sensation. I felt tears trickle down my cheeks. The trickles turned to streams as the strong, cold wind spread them across my face. How could I possibly thank Him enough for what He had done in all of our lives? He had brought our boys home alive!

There we stood in the cold, biting wind, huddled together, arm in arm, all of us, our hearts beating strong, the anxiety in the air increasing, as we anticipated the moment. That moment to lay eyes on his eyes, to have him, to hold him, and embrace him with love and gratitude.

The plane approached slowly and turned in front of us. The doors seemed to take forever to open, though it was probably just a few minutes. Finally, they opened, and out jumped Mask and MeSo! Mask completely bypassed the steps. He must have temporarily forgotten his injured leg. The men went through the receiving line of military brass, and then, finally . . . that moment . . . to have and to hold the sweetness of life itself.

TYLER

Meso and I landed on the twenty-sixth of March back in England on a cold, wet night, with a huge welcoming party and family waiting. It was a great feeling to be back. Immediately, Mom and Dad and I exchanged hugs. Then, through tear-filled eyes, to my utter amazement I saw my brother, Trevor, who was next in line to welcome me home! We all agreed it was worth every bit of the energy it took to arrange for that moment! Priceless!

After the welcome home hugs from family and friends, we all headed back to the suite for some much-needed family time. Though completely exhausted and relieved to be back in London, I shared some highlights of my experience. I, of course, was somewhat limited in what I could share due to the confidentiality issue while the incident was still being investigated. You can imagine, if you choose to eject from a $54 million fighter jet, to have it crash and burn, there will be a multitude of questions and investigations from many departments in the military.

Because of all this, I was allowed to return briefly to my home in Cambridge to shower, change clothes, etc., and then I had to report back to base for the next few days for further debriefings with the Accident Board. The Accident Board findings would eventually show that the plane had a malfunction and was not shot down by enemy fire.

Welcome home!

Reunited with family.

Group photo with family and friends.

REFLECTION

By the touch of His hand, God moved us like pawns, to exactly the right position at exactly the right time. His presence was everywhere! He always delivers! He's never a minute early. He's never a minute late. The key in allowing it all to happen His way is *trusting* Him enough to let it all go.

Faith ~ Fear ~ Freedom

Having a little *faith* releases *fear*, releasing *fear* is finding *freedom*.

chapter eleven

TIMELY MEETINGS

To everything there is a season, a time for every purpose under heaven; a time to be born, and a time to die; a time to plant, and a time to pluck what is planted; a time to kill, and a time to heal; a time to break down, and a time to build up.

ECCLESIASTES 3:1-3 NKJV

DORENE

At this point, we had not picked up the rental car yet, which was still waiting for us in Cambridge, so Trevor and Tyler decided to hop the train back to Cambridge for the night. Tyler had to report back to base Sunday morning, earlier than the rental car company opened, so Trevor would be operating solo while trying to get to the car rental, pick up the car, and navigate his way back to the base. This would be his first experience driving on the left side of the road while steering from the right side of the van. He was completely on his own, without a cell phone, no GPS, and in a strange land. *Good luck with that one buddy, but we are counting on you!*

We then realized Trevor did not have a pass to get on base. No one was available to assist with this piece, so off we went to talk to the gate guards about the situation. Just so happens, they were waiting for the arrival of a four-star general to award someone with a purple heart. Security was heightened for the pomp and circumstance, and the base was quite engaged in activity.

In spite of all that, we explained our dilemma to the gate guards, who were more than helpful in assisting us after we provided the necessary security information. We can't say enough about the first-class treatment we received from every individual we came in contact with on the base.

After about an hour's wait and right on time, Trevor showed up at the gate. What an amazing job of navigating! We were excited to get our day under way, so we hopped in the van and took off for a day of sightseeing and lunch in the neighboring town of Newmarket. Later, Trevor and Tyler drove back to Cambridge for some additional brother-bonding time.

Monday morning, we happened to meet up with the colonel at breakfast, and he extended an invitation for us to visit the control tower. Of course, we jumped right on that offer! It was quite the experience for the five of us civilians to watch the Strike Eagle formations taking off and landing. The power surge, of feeling the earth tremble and the atmosphere vibrate around you truly was a WOW moment. Something we will never forget.

Monday evening, we all (Bruce, Trevor, Mike, Paula, and I) drove up to Cambridge, as we were to meet Kelly Prosser, Tyler's girlfriend, for the first time. She had not seen Tyler since his return from Libya, so we knew this would be a lovely reunion for them.

Tyler met Kelly in the States before he departed from Seymour Johnson AFB in North Carolina. Another moment of divine design. Kelly, who lived in Essex, England, was visiting a friend in North Carolina. Originally, she had purchased plane tickets to see a friend in Hawaii. Well, as God would have it, Kelly's plans to go to Hawaii fell through, and so she had a ticket to the States that she wasn't sure how to use. In expressing her frustration about the dilemma to her friend in North Carolina, she was extended an invitation to go visit. Kelly accepted the invite! After the airport pick-up, Kelly and her friend made their way to a bar in Raleigh, North Carolina. Tyler's "bros" had arranged a going away party for him at the same bar in celebration of his assignment to the Royal AFB in Lakenheath, England.

Tyler and Kelly "randomly" met in this bar and began talking. Like the movie *Top Gun*, boy meets girl in a bar.

Tyler, of course, noticing her lovely British accent, inquired as to where she lived and her history there.

She had lived there all her life and knew the surroundings quite well, of course. When Tyler disclosed he was headed to the UK himself, Kelly graciously extended her assistance in helping him get acquainted when he arrived and shared her contact info with him. (With a big grin on her face, Kelly told me when we met, "You know, Mum, I could have given him the wrong number but I didn't.")

Tyler and Kelly.

Well, Tyler is wise and when God sends a gift of opportunity and guidance he is not going to pass up the offer. So, sure enough, he rang her up when he arrived in London, and she arranged a meeting place at the train station. True to her word (which is who Kelly is), the two semi-strangers met, and she began the first of many "educational tours" around London, advising him about where he might want to live. As it turned out, three years later, with a one-year military extension in England, our USAF F-15 Strike Eagle Navigator WSO was wed to the lovely lady from Essex, England (a senior advisor within the Kennel Club in Piccadilly Square, London). The wedding was held on March 13, 2014, at the lovely Rowton Castle. Once again, divine design.

We all shared a wonderful evening over dinner in Cambridge and enjoyed a romantic walk along the River Thames that night. In the tranquility of the still air and calm water of the river, we quietly soaked up a moment of gratitude. A time to briefly reflect within ourselves the challenges we had faced and the blessings we were living in that moment together. It was that gentle *peace* that welled up inside of me. Here I was, with my loving husband, our two sons, our very dear friends, alive, together, in England, following a very emotional year with my parents. (The story of my parents can be found in the "Moments in Time-Evidence of God" section under "Reconciliation.")

MASK ATTEMPTED TO EXPLAIN
THE UNEXPLAINABLE—
A PEACE THAT CAME
OVER HIM, COMFORT AND
CALMNESS IN THE MIDST
OF UNCERTAINTY.

chapter 12

WELCOME HOME CEREMONY

Where we love is home,
home that our feet may leave, but not our hearts.

OLIVER WENDELL HOLMES, SR.

DORENE

To honor the return of MeSo and Mask, the base quickly arranged a Yellow Ribbon Ceremony. Trevor was supposed to fly back the day prior; however, not wanting to miss such an important celebration for his brother, he once again put his job on the line. He requested an additional day off that he hadn't yet earned. Fortunately, a not-so-understanding supervisor finally agreed to let him stay just one more day. Trevor would have walked off that job if it meant missing this! Thank God for His goodness in touching cold hearts. He always takes care of the details!

The ceremony was held inside one of the hangers on base. With the wing commander and more than a thousand service members present and with an F-15E as the backdrop, we were honored to be escorted to the front row.

After an introduction and a brief summary of the event, MeSo and Mask were given the opportunity to say a few words. Again, due to the confidentiality of the situation, they were quite limited in what they could share. After a wonderful round of applause in recognition of

MeSo and Mask preparing to deliver their experiences.

their return home, MeSo took the podium and expressed the fear that came over him as he experienced what he thought was as close to dying as he had ever been. MeSo experienced a "traditional" series of events from hitting the ground to rescue. The moment his feet hit the ground, he started to evade from everyone around him to ensure safe recovery. While there was protection overhead for most of his time on the ground, there were several moments in which he felt he might not make it home. Those were his toughest moments, as he wanted to make sure that those who were airborne overhead passed on his message of love to his wife. He overcame many close moments as he was being chased until he was picked up by helicopter and taken to safety on a US Navy ship.

Here is another piece of irony. About two months after the incident, Trevor was sharing Tyler's situation with a close friend of his. During their conversation, she mentioned that at the time Tyler's plane went down, her husband, a naval officer, was on deployment in the Middle East. By coincidence (or perhaps not), he was on the night shift when Mask was in peril. He saw a banner come over his computer screen about "Mask Stark" being involved in the incident in Libya.

He recognized the last name but could not place it; however, his wife could, and she reminded him who Mask was. It has become a very small world, even when it's half a world away! What are the odds?

Mask was up next and gave a brief summary of his capture by the local rebels. He explained how the shepherd's dog had sniffed him out, and then, he heard men approaching him, where he sat behind a bush. Initially, there was no way of knowing if these men and woman

Mask at the podium.

were friend or foe. The difference in Mask's and Meso's stories was quite evident. MeSo's experience was based on emotion, uncertainty, and running for his life, while Mask attempted to explain the unexplainable—a peace that came over him, comfort and calmness in the midst of uncertainty. Capture or rescue, this peace stayed with him throughout all of these unknowns. *I believe this peace was the result of our prayer warriors in action.*

He publicly gave credit where credit was due and honored God in doing so. He also passed along his gratitude to the numerous military personnel who were involved in his rescue and safe return to Lakenheath. This took some courage for Mask, as it might for any of us. This was the first opportunity in his life to make such a public stand for God and to give God the honor and glory for his life. Not only that, but now that Mask had opened this door publicly, it prompted MeSo to call up enough courage to rise to the podium for a second time to honor God and those in the military as well. Are we more concerned about doing the popular thing or the right thing? Every choice we make matters. These two stood up for the right thing!

God is not as concerned about where you are going but rather who you are becoming. This is why we are called to STAND and be a witness, so others may know the wonders of God.

Many, O LORD my God, are the wonderful works which You have done, And Your thoughts toward us; There is none to compare with You. If I would declare and speak of your wonders, they would be too many to count.

PSALM 40:5 AMP

Welcome Home Mask and MeSo!

Ana, MeSo,
Mask,
Dorene,
Bruce,
and Trevor.

Military
brass.

Bruce, Dorene,
Mask, Trevor,
Paula, and Mike.

REFLECTION

Is this not the power of prayer that brought Mask his peace? Mask felt the blanket of protection and God's presence embrace him in every moment, no matter what came. This was how God answered the requests of our prayer warriors. God has asked us all to pray for each other, to support, protect, heal, and encourage. Our prayers never go unheard, and He will always honor our obedience in a way only He knows to be the perfect outcome. We must trust. He also asks that we let go and give Him the moments of our day. I believe without a doubt that *trusting* and being *obedient* in completely giving back my son, along with numerous prayers, resulted in not only saving Mask's life, but it also allowed both of us to experience the embrace of unexplainable peace during such an emotional time. This was the peace the lieutenant colonel could sense on the phone.

All these blessings shall come upon you and overtake you, because you obey the voice of the LORD your God.

DEUTERONOMY 28:2 NKJV

After the ceremony, we gathered in front of the commander's plane for some pictures and engaged in conversations with the military brass that had helped us along the way.

Suggestions came up about meeting for dinner and other ideas about socializing later in the evening. The commander had suggested we all meet in Cambridge for drinks at his favorite bar. He and his wife had arranged for a sitter for their children and were looking forward to their "date night." Unsure how to answer, I told him I would get back to him after we had spoken with Tyler. When I relayed the invitation to Tyler, he was really uncomfortable with the idea of drinking with the boss. Tyler was also concerned that he would be pressed to get there by train on time. To not be timely when meeting your commander by special invitation would be very disrespectful. To complicate matters, we would not be able to go with Tyler since we needed to return our rental car first and then take a cab to meet them. We were going to be late as well! Understandably, none of this sat well with Tyler, as now he was meeting his colonel one on one! To add to the stress, Tyler met with some additional roadblocks along the way. Wouldn't it be just like the Adversary to try to prevent, or at least complicate, a lovely plan?

Well, God is always up to something! *If we can just come to trust that He is in every moment and live in the presence of that moment, His divine design always has a purpose and, in the end, will always prevail.* God arranged for this meeting between Tyler and his commander for the opportunity to have a more intimate conversation. Though the conversation was not shared, Tyler expressed his gratitude on multiple occasions for the valuable time spent with his commander that otherwise might not have happened. God is in the details! Awareness is the key!

Thanking Him always for every moment, whether it makes sense or not, whether we understand it or not, is essential in allowing God to do His best work. We need to stay out of His way.

He that trusteth in his own heart is a fool: but whoso walketh wisely, he shall be delivered.

PROVERBS 28:26

After our delayed arrival to the pub, we all enjoyed a drink and some conversation. The commander told the story about receiving my email about Tyler's endangerment shortly after his capture. He relayed his astonishment around that email and how unlikely it was to have received it. "I was completely baffled by it and didn't know how to respond to it, so I simply didn't." It was a great story to hear. At this time, the commander locked eyes with Bruce and stated with deliberate frankness, "I am not sure you realize how fortunate you are that your son is still here." The intensity of his statement took Bruce quite by surprise. The commander was right. As grateful as we felt, we did not have many, many details about the ejection, the capture, the rescue, and the return. We had no details around the dangers he faced and the protection he received. Once again, it brought the message to our hearts that we were living God's divine design.

The commander had made a reservation for us at his favorite restaurant next door. Sadly, he was not able to join us, due to time restrictions with the sitter. We so would have loved to sit with him for a while, though it must not have been meant to be. The lieutenant colonel, however, did manage to meet up with us for dinner as a surprise guest, and it was a pleasure spending time and getting to know him briefly as well.

Enjoying a dinner together.

The lieutenant colonel and Tyler stayed by themselves after dinner, so they, too, were able to enjoy some time in a private conversation. Once again, Tyler expressed his gratitude for how this evening had been arranged so perfectly for him in the end.

Putting faces to the names of the people who were so instrumental in keeping us informed and assisting us through this process was a blessing in itself.

Touring London

Several days later, Tyler was given a respite from his military duties and so was able to spend a few days with us to recover a little bit and to clear his mind. We arranged to meet Kelly, gather up Mike and Paula, and off we went on our touring adventures in London. Though Tyler's leg was giving him some serious pain, he didn't want to ruin the original plan of the family's first trip to the UK, so we spent the next few days in London with Kelly showing us the sights.

Since this was our first trip ever to the United Kingdom, we of course, were excited to see London, to step away from military events, and to become tourists for awhile.

Of course, sometimes the best laid plans have their own sets of struggles. I have always maintained, "If you have expectations, you're sure to be disappointed. If you have an open mind, you're sure to embrace the gifts." Fortunately for our group, we had all agreed on the "open mind" theory, which always proves to be the better option.

Tyler and Kelly's enthusiasm for touring London was admirable. There was certainly no shortage of wonderful pubs where we could rest our weary feet, share many a raised glass, and toast the path we had just been on and the moments we were in. We shared some much-needed laughter as well.

Underneath the laughter, we were all experiencing the need for an inner release as we reflected on the emotional roller-coaster ride we had just been on together, especially Tyler. This picture of Tyler and Kelly needs no further explanation.

"Good-bye."

It seemed as though we had been in a time warp, and it was now time to focus on the trip back home. It was a bittersweet moment, as we attempted to sort through so many emotions: rejoicing in the gift of standing on that tarmac, embracing the life of our rescued son, and now having to say "good-bye" and return to life as we knew it.

There is no turning back. We were all touched by His hand. We were all changed in different ways. We were not the same, though our story had a beautiful ending.

*A new day will dawn on us from above
because our God is loving and merciful.*

LUKE 1:78 GW

REFLECTION

With a heavy heart. I ask you to remember the countless other families whose lives have also been changed as a result of their sacrifice. Please pause here for a moment and pray with me for the numerous military families whose stories often end in tragedy. They gave their best. They gave their all. They paid the highest price. They gave their life! Again, *freedom is not free.*

No matter your faith or your religion, you may join me, or perhaps you would prefer your own private offering. It doesn't matter. Send those hurting families your heart, your love, and your gratitude, for the freedoms you enjoy every day in your life.

Lord, God Almighty, with the power that you hold and the love that you give, we ask for a blanket of protection and healing to help heal and console the mind, body, and spirit of all those affected within the military and for the selfless acts of sacrifice they perform on a daily basis. We want to honor their passion for their country and their courage to protect it with our deepest gratitude.

In Jesus, in love,
Your Prayer Warriors

MY HEART JUST MELTED.
IT WAS AS IF THE LORD HAD
PICKED ME UP AND LITERALLY
HELD ME IN HIS ARMS TO SAY,
"I'VE GOT THIS."

chapter 13

GOD MOVES THE MOUNTAIN

---

*He replied, "Because you have so little faith.
Truly I tell you, if you have faith as small
as a mustard seed, you can say to this mountain,
'Move from here to there,' and it will move.
Nothing will be impossible for you."*

MATTHEW 17:20

DORENE

Shortly after our return home in March, Tyler informed us that he would be preparing for another deployment in May. This time to South Korea. This was quite concerning to his mother's heart. In my maternal opinion, much healing still needed to take place on every level before moving him forward into another dangerous position, yet I understood from my own life with horses, that any traumatic incident required a remount as soon as possible. I knew he must "get back in the saddle" again, which he did. Yet, something felt very unsettling to me for reasons I really cannot explain. Yes, the pit in my stomach returned. So, as is my routine, I would again consult the Divine and come to Him with the desires of my heart.

> *Lord, we have come this far, and I am feeling like Tyler's healing is not enough in his mind, body, and spirit, and his confidence has been shaken. The possibility of going into battle yet again, just doesn't feel very settling. I once again trust him in your care to hold him, heal him, and care for him. He is yours. I will be watching and waiting for your divine design to bring the perfect healing before he re-enters a deployment situation.*

Following my prayer request, it was not long before Tyler communicated that his deployment to Korea had been postponed due to some interesting circumstances. Coincidence? My heart just melted. It was as if the Lord had picked me up and literally held me in His arms to say, "I've got this." The joy and peace that flowed into me cannot be described in words.

REFLECTION

I feel the need to reiterate here: we are children of God and heirs to the throne. Our Heavenly Father has requested that we approach Him and ask for what we desire in our hearts. If it aligns with His will, those requests will be granted. The key here is *we need to ask*. Whether we are asking for answers or asking for gifts, we are not ready to receive until we first ask. Otherwise, how are we able to recognize the answer and give gratitude to the Giver?

First – Identify the need

    Second – Recognize the gift

        Third – Honor God with the gift

So I say to you: Ask and it will be given to you; seek and you will find; knock and the door will be opened to you. For everyone who asks receives; the one who seeks finds; and to the one who knocks, the door will be opened.
Which of you fathers, if your son asks for a fish, will give him a snake instead?
Or if he asks for an egg, will give him a scorpion?

> *If you then, though you are evil, know how to give good gifts to your children, how much more will your Father in heaven give the Holy Spirit to those who ask Him!*
>
> LUKE 9:11–13

When I have those quiet moments in between the chaos of life (seems like mostly in the shower or in the car), I have some of my best conversations with God. I'm sure I'm not the only one who speaks to God in this manner; it's just something none of us seem to talk about. Well, given the current situation, I had an immediate flashback to one of those conversations that had taken place shortly after Tyler's return from Libya. I was in the shower. *God, you always talk about having faith. I know what faith is, but how do you measure it? How do we know if we have enough? I think I have faith, but if it really came down to it—a life or death situation—would I have the faith or the courage to stand up and die for Christ? There are individuals all over the world and throughout history that have, and still are, dying in the name of Christ. How much faith do I have?* His scripture came rushing through my mind about the faith of a mustard seed.

———————∽———————

He put another parable before them, saying,
"The kingdom of heaven is like a grain of mustard seed
that a man took and sowed in his field.
It is the smallest of all seeds, but when it has
grown it is larger than all the garden plants
and becomes a tree, so that the birds of the air
come and make nests in its branches."

MATTHEW 13:31-32 ESV

————————————————

I thought, *Okay then, I haven't moved any mountains.* So, it's clear to me my faith is smaller than the smallest of seeds. "How much do I have? How can I measure how much I have? Can He show me some way, somehow? How do I get more?" Questions like these continued to come into my mind. I asked. He delivered! Of course!

Take a breath. *He moved the mountain!*

A mother's heart once again consoled in the arms of our Lord. Here is how He moved that mountain.

South Korea Deployment

Tyler returned to work immediately following our visit and was classified as "Duties Not to Include Flying." This is his account of what followed.

TYLER

The military needed to move a fleet of twelve jets, along with flight crews, from England to Hawaii. Someone was needed to plan jet recovery at the necessary Air Force bases, as well as lodging reservations and coordinating logistics with South Korea. Since I was unable to fly, I had a lot of free time, so they decided to use me in this capacity. Mind you, a desk job would not be high on my list of favorite jobs. I would find out later how fortunate I was to have been given this appointment.

I was assigned to Hawaii while overseeing these logistics. It was to be a short-term, seven-day undertaking. The jets were to fly from England to Mountain Home, Idaho, then Mountain Home to Hawaii. I had worked diligently to coordinate all of these pieces to flow in an efficient manner for all twelve planes and crews.

Shortly after my arrival in Hawaii to oversee this endeavor, an unlikely event occurred. *A volcano erupted in Iceland!* Obviously, this had a very negative impact on our military plan.

Now, due to the heavy ash in the atmosphere, the jets that were to fly from England to Mountain Home were grounded! This created a domino effect, because now the fuel tankers that were scheduled to be a huge part of this massive fleet movement, were now having to be rescheduled for other duties. It also meant our scheduled support had been lost. As a result of this *shaking Iceland mountain*, our window of opportunity had now closed. Instead of taking seven to eight days, the trip from England to Korea, going west, ended up taking forty-two days to get all twelve jets two-thirds of the way around the world. Now, we had jets scattered all over the place due to maintenance issues and tanker non-availability. We ended up having jets in Iceland; Goose Bay, Canada; Seymour Johnson; Mountain Home; Hawaii; Guam; and South Korea.

While the schedule was in constant flux with jet arrival times changing on a daily basis, which meant adjusting car rental and room reservations regularly, there was a fair amount of downtime. This allowed me and the three other guys that were part of the team to explore the island. We sampled many beach bars, took advantage of happy hours, and swam with sea turtles while snorkeling. Certain nights our biggest problem was, do we have sushi or hit up the local bar for a good burger? Decisions, decisions! I am not sure what path my healing would have taken without this amazing gift of downtime, in one of God's many beautiful locations. The slow pace helped me recoup after a very emotional few months of recovering and readjusting, on every level. My leg had even healed.

In the end, we had jets break down in Hawaii, and they sat idle for so long, a test flight was now required before continuing the journey to South Korea. By this point, the Air Force had now cleared me to fly, and I felt I was healed enough that it was time to get back in the cockpit again. What better way would there be to reacquaint myself with the jet and, more importantly, to sit in an ejection seat again, than doing an island tour of Hawaii? I took my first test flight. It felt great to reconnect with the jet again. It was just what I needed to get my confidence back to fly. I will always be grateful for this gift of time and renewal.

REFLECTION

Here we are, just a couple of weeks following my conversation with God about my faith. With Tyler's phone call from Hawaii, God literally took my breath away. After hanging up the phone and absorbing what had just transpired, I realized that God had once again brought me to my knees. They honestly buckled from beneath me as I reached for the chair in front of me. I was completely awestruck. He overwhelms me with His grace and love. His faithfulness is flawless, His peace beyond measure. Not only had he honored my request for additional healing time for Tyler, He chose to bring it in a manner that would also answer my question of faith. In this quiet moment, immersed in the "reflection of perfection," He brought that gentle voice: "If you have the faith of a mustard seed you can ask the mountain to move, and it will move." I felt as if He was saying, "Let me show you how this works." Yes, of course, I cried again.

> Tyler was now completely healed and ready for South Korea after having been given the gift of a month in Hawaii. It allowed him the time he needed to be healed spiritually and mentally.

DORENE

War Tours and the Mask

Tyler served his time in South Korea and then returned to England. He was then called upon to do a "War Tour" in the United States. This would involve touring some of the Air Force bases to give talks about his experience. He would be allowed to share new knowledge about what went wrong, what went right, and add some new dynamics to their training. He has mentioned countless times the effort, manpower, and importance the military had put on his rescue. He truly felt they had made his life their highest priority, and he regularly expresses how grateful he is for their care and concern for himself and for Meso. Their families share in that gratitude.

An Air Force pilot relayed it to me this way:

You know, when you sit in those classes and listen to all of the safety plans and procedures, you tend to think, "Oh, this would never really happen, and if it did, it certainly wouldn't happen to me." Your mind begins to wander, and you tend to lose focus. Listening to Tyler tell his story brought it to life right in front of us. Then you start thinking, this really can happen, did happen, and yes, it could happen to anyone, including me! It made me realize the importance of our training. I am a better pilot today because of his story. It really shifted my thinking. I once thought I was invincible in the jet. Now I know I'm not. I have a different respect for the jet and for flying because of someone who actually lived through it and was willing to tell his story. Please thank him for his service.

Again, I believe if you can make a difference in just one life, it is worth having gone through the experience.

It was during these "War Tours" that Tyler would gather more information from the Air Force regarding the misprogramming of the radios and why he had no communication with his base. He would learn about how closely Gaddafi's men were following him and why they had to move him thirteen times in three days. Not an easy task. To think, without any initial communication with his base and without the help of those amazing people, how easy it would have been for Tyler to be captured.

It was our visit with Michael Lewis when we learned a few more interesting pieces around the event. He explained that his source told him Gaddafi's men were scouring villages and knocking on doors in search of the "French" pilot of the now-burning plane. They even visited the house where Tyler had been taken, but by then, he had been removed. He claimed that the people there lied to Gaddafi's men, stating they had not seen the pilot. The risk they had taken in harboring Tyler, even for a short time, could have cost them their lives. God in action again!

The Lord will grant that the enemies
who rise up against you will be defeated before you.
They will come at you from one direction
but flee from you in seven.

DEUTERONOMY 28:7

Michael also informed us that a gentleman in Libya was in possession of Tyler's helmet and mask. His intention was to return that mask to Tyler by way of his parents. He purchased tickets to the United States to surprise them with this prized possession. Unfortunately, for reasons we may never know, his piece of luggage that contained the mask never made it to his transfer in Turkey. Without the mask, there was no purpose for him to continue the trip, so he flew back home. We were left to wonder if perhaps the mask had been stolen. Though we were heartbroken that the opportunity to meet him and hold Tyler's mask had passed us by, we were more saddened we missed that moment to show him our deepest gratitude for his thoughtfulness and his efforts. I would imagine the time and expense would have had an impact on him. What an amazing heart! It's one thing to think about it, but quite another to actually follow through. And, to think, he didn't even realize how symbolic this mask would be for us, with Tyler's call sign being "Mask." God bless him.

The story would still end beautifully, though. When we shared this new disclosure to Tyler, he was completely taken aback. "Wow," he replied, "I actually have the mask! I had recently received an email with a request for some Air Force patches and coins in exchange for the mask. Of course, I delivered, and so did he. We never kept in contact, as it seemed through the tone of the email, he just wanted a simple exchange and that was all."

chapter 14

IN THE STILLNESS

Be still and know that I am God;
I will be exalted among the nations,
I will be exalted in the earth.

PSALM 46:10

DORENE

We have shared our family stories in hopes it will help you find your own blessings in your own events. Perhaps in your reflection of these events, you can see the perfection and intervention of God's divine design in your own life. Sometimes it is so easy to claim coincidence or look the other way because His touch was so subtle. Are you keeping God at arm's length? You don't need to love God from a distance. He longs for an intimate relationship with you, a relationship that can be found only through Jesus. Dare yourself to reach out and grab His hand—one of God's most profound requests . . . that took me so long to learn.

It is not how much time you spend in the Bible or how many scriptures you have memorized. It's the time you spend with Him in stillness. Sadly, we are often strangers to stillness.

It is the relationship you feel in your heart for Him that He desires most. It is your love He longs for.

It is in the *quiet* moments of our lives, in the time we have set aside just for Him, in silence, that He longs for. His desire is for you to bring your heart. No words necessary, just your heart. You see, He already knows what is in your heart.

Only a *quiet mind* . . .
 and a *quiet heart* . . .
  are able to hear the *quiet whisper* of our Lord.
   Allow yourself to just *be* in His presence.
    To just be *held* in His arms.

Ten minutes, just ten minutes a day with Him, will change your life. The devil will try to talk you out of it from every angle. *Don't be fooled!* He comes to steal your joy!

Finding stillness with God is an art. Perfecting an art takes discipline. The more you practice, the deeper the love. The deeper the love, the deeper the desire. This is where the blessings are bestowed upon you.

> Stillness invites the relationship.
> The relationship invites intimacy.
> Intimacy invites peace, joy, and wisdom.

I encourage you to ask yourself: "What do I really have to do in my life, in this moment, that could possibly be more important than five or ten minutes with my *God*?" Those will be your most cherished moments. *Fight* for them!

YOU are the treasure He is seeking!

His love will fill you up with whatever you need for the rest of the day. *Trust Him. He loves you.* If you have said "yes" to Jesus—His crucifixion and resurrection—then His Spirit lives inside of you. His Spirit is *love*. Yes, this means you, too, are *love*. Now, we are all one in the body. How are you growing it? How are you sharing it? How are you living it? Are you standing in your sacred truth, living for who God created you to be?

---ˢ---

These things I have spoken unto you,
that in me ye might have peace.
In the world ye shall have tribulation:
but be of good cheer; I have overcome the world.

JOHN 16:33

Are you choosing *all of Him*?
  Or just the pieces you want?
    Are you giving *all of you*?
      Or just the pieces you want?
        Is this a pure and honest love?
          A complete relationship?
            Or are you loving with conditions?

Our relationship with Jesus is entirely up to us. He is already all in. He has already proved His pure love, to the point of death. In the depth of your soul, are you being honest with yourself? "Who am I, really? Am I all in?" You were created for every moment you have been given. Who are you today? Who will you be tomorrow?

Everyone is born with a gift, a purpose; whether it is small or large is insignificant. As it is in nature, from the smallest to the largest all have a purpose. As do we in the body. Honor the gifts you have been given by nurturing them and loving them as you come to love yourself more fully.

Where is your heart taking you? What are your dreams, your desires, your passions? What is holding you back? God loathes lukewarm believers. Are you still on the fence? Jump one way or the other, but *choose*! Sitting on the fence goes nowhere! *Jump!* Now, putting aside all fear that the devil has put before you, where is your heart taking you? Who's stopping you now? Only by surrendering to Truth, will you find the Way. Once you are *all in*, you will become *unstoppable*! He will guide your every step with wisdom and strength to move forward. Dare yourself to be brave enough to reach out and grab His hand.

The LORD shall fight for you,
and ye shall hold your peace.

EXODUS 14:14

Prayer for Our Military and Their Families

Heavenly Father,

We do not underestimate Your love and power in our lives, nor in the lives of those who sacrifice themselves for our freedom every day. You have foreseen what lies ahead for many warriors and their families. Today, we ask you to cover them with a blanket of protection, just as you have done and continue to do for our family. We ask,

Father, for you to walk side by side, in step with every warrior, whether over land or over sea. Shield them with Your mighty hands. While they are away, please hold tight the hearts and hands of loved ones waiting for their return home. Magnify your presence in their lives with your peace and love, especially those who have turned their hearts away from you.

Thank you, Jesus. Amen.

———— ✐ ————

If you have made a separation,
do you understand why?

Are you the lost sheep our Shepherd seeks,
the one that makes Him cry?

How many times will you choose
to turn your back when you hear His voice?

What causes you to hesitate
in making a clear choice?

How many times will He seek you out?

Perhaps it is more than you're willing to count?

DORENE STARK

————————

Bring your secrets to the cross.
Grace is on the other side.

UNKNOWN

I do not understand the mystery of grace—
only that it meets us where we are
and does not leave us where it found us.

ANNE LAMOTT

You say you don't see God in your life?
Perhaps you're just not looking.

DORENE STARK

The Great I AM

I walk in front, I walk behind,
My love surrounds you from all sides.
Patiently, I wait to see
That moment you will notice me.

To be your best friend
In all that you do,
Therein lies the purpose
I created in you.

You say your life
Just happens by chance,
When in fact it's designed
For your knowing glance.

For you to seek me
And desire my love
Is the sweetness of life
I bring down from above.

Be still and be present,
My Spirit in man,
Be held in the arms,
Of the Great I Am.

DORENE STARK

AFTERWORD

• • •

THE FIRST ACCOUNT
NOT AS BRIEFED

By Melvin Stark

(Bruce Stark's father/Tyler Stark's grandfather)

Bold text signifies similarities between Tyler's experiences and those of his grandfather in World War II.

Yes, on every bombing mission we were briefed for what we might encounter from the enemy, but on this one, most of it we were not briefed for. It all started on July 26, 1944, while flying north of Vienna, on our way to bomb an aircraft plant in Wiener Neustadt, Austria. We were flying out of Foggia, **Italy**, with the 15th Air Force. I was the right waist machine-gunner in a crew of ten. The Luftwaffe had given us a vacation for quite a while, so we were without escort today (our guys were on the Eastern Front doing strafing for the Russians). We were flying Tail-End Charlie and were the most vulnerable in a formation. We were about thirty minutes from the target when the tail gunner shouted over the intercom that he had spotted enemy fighters at six o'clock low. Before we knew what had happened, our plane started to develop holes from their accurate shooting. I was able to get in one big burst of .50 caliber, but the sun was so bright I could hardly see them making passes at us. When I *could* see, it seemed as if the whole sky was full of planes.

In all the confusion, I can remember something **hitting me in the chest** and knocking me around the ball turret, but not hurting me because I had my flak suit on. When I landed, I was sitting in the radio room with my feet on the ball turret. Although stunned, I made my way back to my gun. The left waist gunner's position was just opposite mine.

As I got to my gun, a rocket knocked a hole, about two feet in diameter, in the side of the plane to my left and landed on the floor between Andy (the left waist gunner) and myself. All I can remember is telling Andy to step on it, and before we knew what happened, the rocket blew up! I must have shielded my face with my right hand because, later on, I realized I was hit with fragments in seventeen places, all up and down my right side and face. The shrapnel severely pierced my right leg, where it imbedded itself and caused excessive bleeding. My intercom and oxygen must have been disconnected when I

Preparing for departure.

got hit because I didn't hear anything from any of the other boys. I did not know just what happened to Andy, but I do remember him saying something about **bailing out** and trying to make his way to the side door. Kicking it out into the open space, he fell by the open wait door. We both must have been hit pretty hard, but at times like this, you just can't remember everything. **All at once, the plane went into a spin, and of course I was thinking of bailing out myself!** The plane was so full of holes you could see the clear blue sky almost any place you looked. I knew my harness was tucked safely away in the basket for empty shells below my gun, easy to get to, **but with the force of the plane in the spin, it was hard to move about.**

Finally, the plane leveled off a bit. I was able to reach for my chute, and oh, what a mess! Ammunition boxes, clothes, and everything were just scattered all over the plane. It is a wonder we didn't get hit on the head with all that junk flying around. I got my chute on my back and had one side snapped on when that crazy plane went into another spin. Once again, the force was so great I just couldn't get the other side snapped on.

Right there, in that situation, was the first time I was ready to give up hope of any chance of getting out of the plane. *I started to pray.* To my surprise, the plane leveled off a little, and I was able to get the other part of my chute snapped on and made my way to the door through all of the rubbish. **I did not see Andy again** after seeing him laying at the side door. I presumed he must have rolled out the open door. Do not know why, but I sat in the doorway with my back to the sky and fell out, pulling the rip cord. The last I remembered was the shroud line coming out of the chute, and then, I blacked out.

We were flying about twenty-seven thousand feet that day. It was a good thing, having all that altitude to fool around in. When I came to, I must have been two to three thousand feet from the ground. It was a **very still day, and my chute seemed to hang in the air.** I looked up

Melvin at right waist gunner post.

and could see parts of planes falling all around me. Later on, I learned 150 German fighters hit us, and we were the first plane to get hit. Out of a squadron of ten planes, only one plane got back to Italy, and all received the Distinguished Flying Cross (an award given to those who perform acts of valor while flying), although there were only two alive to talk about it. **One of those was me.**

As my feet were about to hit the tops of the tall pine trees, a German plane came over and made one pass at me, firing for all he was worth! The trees saved me because I fell through the tops of them and hung about twenty feet from the ground. There I hung between four tall trees, not able to get out of the chute. Oh, was it tight around the crotch! I got myself swinging enough to clamp my legs around one of the trunks but couldn't get my chute off because I was getting so weak from the loss of blood. Finally, I remembered I had put my pocketknife in the leg of my flight suit. *Never before had I taken a knife along!* I got my knife and cut the lines loose.

As I started to slide down the tree, the branches were always in the way, and I was getting so weak, I lost my hold. **I fell to the ground, with the chute coming down on top of me. Darn near smothered me to death!** The first thing I could think of was to find out how bad I was hit. I got out of the flight suit and realized that above my knee and thigh, the blood was just shooting out. I made tourniquets out of two handkerchiefs I had with me and finally stopped the bleeding. I had been hit through the nose with a piece of metal about the size of a wooden match stick. My face being so full of blood, the flies were just sticking to me, and when I tried to breathe through my mouth, they would get in. I was spitting them out like tobacco.

Well, there I was, with the bleeding stopped, but didn't know what to do because every time I would start to move, the bleeding would start all over again. I could hear water running and remembered in briefing they always told us if we wanted help, to follow a stream because people usually lived along a stream. **Unable to walk, I crawled about a block to a clearing, where there was nothing but tree stumps left from someone's cutting. I could see a house about two blocks away on a steep hill.** I knew I couldn't make it up the hill by myself, so I held onto the stumps and hollered for all I was worth. **I needed help, and there was no chance of escape in the condition I was in.**

Pretty soon, here came two young boys who I thought were going to help me, but all they did was stand there and look at me. They didn't know what to do. They wouldn't carry anything except my clothes, so **I began to crawl towards the house** and, on the way, came to a brook. I was so dry I laid face down in the water and drank to my heart's content.

Finally, the boys reached out to help me get to the hut on the hill. I sat down on a bench by the wall. There was an elderly lady and a middle-aged lady. They just stood there and looked at me. I took off all my clothes, except my shorts, wanting to stop the bleeding, but got so weak

Bruce and Tyler on the hill where large portions of Melvin's plane were found.

I started to pass out. I put my head between my knees to get circulation in my head and then laid out on the floor. Finally, they put another bench along the one I sat on and made a bed out of it. They were peasants and very much afraid of me. One of the boys got some straw out of the barn, which was attached to the house, and put it on the benches.

I tried to get them to get a doctor for me, but they couldn't understand English. I tried to give them the American money I carried in my escape kit, but they

Dorene, Johann, Bruce, Tyler, and Erika at the hut where Melvin was hidden.

Taking a glimpse of the past inside the hut.

wouldn't have anything to do with it. I made pretty good time from when we were attacked because I looked at my watch just before we got hit and it was 11:30 a.m. **Now, here I was in a peasant home somewhere in Austria at 12:00.**

The hut/barn where Melvin was taken.

The flies were on my face so thick that one of the ladies put some cheese cloth on my face to keep them off. From then on, I was like a sideshow at a circus because all afternoon, people came in and picked up the cloth, and all they said was "Americano" and looked sad. After all, they were aiding an "enemy." I continued to ask for a doctor, but to no avail. Finally, an elderly man came in who could speak English. He looked me over and said a doctor would be there about seven.

From then on, I either passed out or went to sleep, but I didn't know what happened until I was awakened by someone picking up the cloth on my face. To my surprise, **there was a cute young gal, (thought for a while I must be in heaven) and, from what I could figure out, she must have been a nurse** because she cleaned me all up, dressed my wounds, and kept pointing to my teeth saying, "Shine." Guess she was not used to seeing good teeth in Austria. I would find out later, one of "the boys" had gone into town to seek out some help. They found Maria, who was the clerk and recorder for the town at the time. She also had some medical background. She cared for me for a time, but years later when I met her, she explained **the government could have removed her from her job and even punished her severely for caring for me.** She needed to report me to the authorities promptly before any questions were put upon her.

While this was going on, there was the usual crowd of onlookers. I didn't know what she was saying, but maybe it was a good thing because all the people were back in the room watching. She became very disgusted and loaded me on a stretcher. What a way to be greeted in a foreign country!

An elderly man, two boys, and "the nurse" carried me for about an hour through the woods. Perhaps she could not get anyone to help her carry me, since they looked at me as an enemy. **From what I could figure out, they were taking me to some place where a car would take me to a hospital.** Several times, they stopped to rest, and the nurse would give me some medicine in a spoon, but it was so horrid, she would pour it on a lump of sugar. I could stand it that way. When we got to the place where we were supposed to meet the car, we met a man. He and "the nurse" got into a terrific argument! Guess he refused to let them use his car as an ambulance, so once again, they lifted the stretcher and carried me until they came to a house where several families lived. Two men who had just come in from the fields carried me up to the second floor and put me in a nice, soft bed. Next to the house was an old waterwheel. Everything was so peaceful. They brought me bread with butter, soup, and coffee, and an elderly lady sat by my bed all night, held my hand, and cried. Thought sure I was dying but didn't feel bad at all. (Perhaps due to the medication "the nurse" had given me.) It all seemed like a dream.

A couple of hours later, a German soldier came and took one of my dog tags and told me **I would be taken to a hospital the next morning at 4:00 a.m. All this time, I didn't know what had happened to the rest of my crew.** In the morning, before the sun came up, two men carried me to some railroad tracks. Soon, a train stopped, and they put me in an open boxcar. One man stayed with me. We rode until the sun came up and finally stopped at a small town. While we were stopped there, two G.I.'s came and carried me to another train. *Here, in another boxcar, I met my ball turret gunner, George Demos.* He was as white as a sheet when he saw me because he thought he was the only one to get out of the plane alive. Later, we learned we were the *only two of* *the ten* to tell the story. He came out of it with a strained back and minor burns on his face. We rode together for another hour and then were taken off the train. There were about ten Americans altogether, all of whom had been shot down the day before. Some of the boys were hurt pretty bad, but not a word out of them.

Several German guards were there and made the boys take turns carrying me to some sort of M.P. station. When the boys were getting tired from carrying me and would slow down, the guards would let them have it with the bayonets on the end of their guns. When we got to the M.P. station, they put all the rest of the men in a dungeon and left me laying out on the stretcher. I had a piece of metal sticking out of my right arm that was bothering me, so I asked one of the young German guards if he could take it out. He got out his knife and cut it out. About that time, the air raid alarms went off. Here came the 15th Air Force overhead on their way to bomb Germany. They had taken a terrific beating the day before. The purr of those engines was sweet music to my ears. **We stayed there until midafternoon when a truck came, and they loaded all of us on.** It was one of those wood-burning jobs and every once in a while, they would have to stop and add wood when we started to lose speed. The roads were so rough, Demos and a couple of other boys had to sit on the stretcher to keep me on the truck. It was a flatbed truck with no box on it.

After riding for about an hour, we came to an airfield near Graz, Austria. Good thing the Germans didn't know about it, but the 15th Air Force had bombed it a week before. Here, we were put in cells. Up to this time, I still hadn't found out just how badly I was hurt, so the best thing to do was ask for a doctor. So, I told the guard I would like to see a doctor. In a few minutes, a soldier came in, so I started to moan, thinking I would get some medical aid. To my surprise, the soldier was a doctor, and he examined me. He didn't say anything, just shook his head and walked out. Boy, I thought sure I wouldn't be helped, but here came two soldiers who loaded me in an ambulance. They took me into Graz to an old school that had been converted into a hospital. I was put on the fourth floor in a large room with about fifteen other POW's, including Americans, Frenchmen, Englishmen, and Australians.

We were well guarded, and my bed was next to a kid, last name of Brown, from Dayton, Ohio. When I first arrived at the hospital, they took me to a small room which had been converted into a dispensary. There I met a young French doctor, an Australian by the name of Joe, and an Englishman named Smitty. They were all POW's and were taking care of the wounded. After putting me on a table, Joe and Smitty held me down while the doctor used a knife and tweezers to remove the metal from my wounds. What a time that was with nothing to deaden the pain! I was certainly glad to get rid of that metal.

I got along fine until one day, my temperature shot up real high, and I was taken to the operating room, where more of the metal was removed. Two tubes were placed in my leg to help drain the wound. Medical aid was minimal, consisting only of bandages made out of paper (later, learned it was toilet paper). The pus was so bad it just soaked up the paper. All they would do was wrap more paper around my leg. New paper was put on maybe twice a week. I guess I was lucky to get that much help because the rest of the hospital was full of wounded Germans, and medical supplies were low. The smell from my leg was so bad I had to keep it covered all the time.

After being on my back for five days, they finally gave me crutches so I could get around a little. We got very little food, consisting mostly of cold potatoes and cucumbers all mixed together in vinegar. Once in a while, we were even able to wash it down with tea! A boy by the name of Vernon Offtenkamp was brought in, though he was not very badly hurt. When I left Demos and the rest of the boys at the airfield, that was the last time I saw him until after the war, when I met him in Chicago. He had been taken to Budapest and had a hard time of it, sweating out the war. On September 14, Vernon and I were told we were going to have to leave because they no longer had enough rooms or medical supplies. I had been out of bed for only five days and wasn't too strong, but Vernon wanted to try to escape, so we saved food for our expedition.

When the day came, we had to walk about two miles to the train station. Boy, I just could hardly make it there. I told him it was impossible for me to try to escape, so he said he would stay with me. Shortly after that decision, we were taken to Frankfurt on the Main. We had two very young guards escorting us to our new home. Somehow, in Frankfurt, our guards took us to the *wrong* railway station. Anyway, there we met five other American flyers who were going to the same place as us. While we were waiting for the guards to make up their minds where to take us, an air raid alarm sounded, and sure enough, here came the US Air Force overhead and bombed a part of the city east of us. We stood there and watched the whole affair. After it was all over and the guards found out where we were supposed to go, we started on our way to the section of the city that had just been bombed. If we had not been taken to the "wrong station," we would have been in the midst of the raid and perhaps died there!

When we arrived at the "right" railway station, it was clear that our bombers had been in the neighborhood! What confusion! People were running in all directions to keep away from the falling and burning roofs. When the civilians saw us with our flying outfits on, they started at us, but the guards kept them off. The people called us "baby killers," "terror flyers," "Chicago gangsters," and so on. In all the confusion, with people running everywhere, we got mixed up in the crowd, and one lady beat the dickens out of me. I got knocked to the ground, and everyone was trampling me. Vernon was next to me and in the mess, too. We now realized we had lost our guards. We finally saw them and crawled over to them to keep the civilians off of us. The guards managed to keep them off and took us to some sort of an M.P. station. Here came the civilians again, determined to get us! Finally, the guards put us behind some large doors and stood there with their guns pointed at the civilians.

After the guards had found out where to take us, we started to walk down the bombed-out streets. Again, the civilians followed us and threw stones at us. When it finally got too bad, the guards stopped a truck and put us on it. Eventually, we stopped at a small rail station, where they put us on a train car with compartments (room enough for about fifteen people), locked the door, and left. Again, the civilians came with a large post and were trying to knock down the door, but the guards stopped them again. Without those guards, we would have surely died!

Next, we went to the small town of Wetzlar, which turned out to be an interrogation center (which we believe to be Dulag Luft).

I was never so glad to be behind barbed wire as then. We were put in a small cell quite infested with bed bugs. After being in there a few hours, a guard came in and sat down and started to talk. While I was in Graz, in the hospital, a French-Canadian priest came in to see me and gave me a prayer book. I had this prayer book on the bed, and when the guard saw it, he picked it up and looked through it and said, "Aw, boy, you Americans believe in a God." He stated that when they bomb and kill people, it wasn't wrong for them because they didn't believe in a God. I was in no position to argue with him, so I forgot about it and asked him if I could see a doctor. He said he would tell the medics and left. Finally, a guard came and told me I could go to the dispensary. The cells were in a long building, with a long hallway, and guards walking up and down the hallway. After I had my bandages changed, I was walking back to my cell when a German soldier approached me and said he was a Catholic priest, and he was going to get me out of there. About that time, a guard came around the corner, so the priest left in a hurry. I never did find out just what he was up to.

I was left alone in my cell for another day and was then taken to a small office, where a German lieutenant sat. The first thing he did was offer me an American cigarette. I told him I didn't want anything he had stolen from an American. He wanted to know what the tail insignia of our squadron was. I wouldn't tell him a thing. I couldn't have anyways because they had changed it about a week before my last mission, and I couldn't have remembered it if I had wanted to. He got disgusted and told me he knew all about me and my crew. He told me where I was born and raised, where I took my training, and the names of all my original crew members. I told him I had been in the hospital for nearly two months. As far as I knew the war could be over. He let me go back to my cell, and in a few days, I was sent to a regular POW camp. This time, I was put in a covered boxcar with so many other men that we were packed in like sardines. Enough room to stand, but not move. I am not sure how long the train ride was, but I will never forget the misery of it. It was hot and the car had no ventilation; we were thirsty and sweating, but there was no water. We began getting dehydrated and had to resort to *drinking our own urine* in order to stay alive. If we wanted to rest our legs, we would have to lay on top of each other, as there was not enough room to sit down. It was a grueling ride to the POW camp, but somehow, we all survived. This was where I stayed until we were liberated on Mother's Day, May 13, 1945, by the Russians.

These are just a few of the experiences *not* covered in our briefings, and very little prepared me for my experiences during the ten months of the POW camp. The documentaries you see and hear about are true. The men you see walk into the "showers" and never return—it's true. The stench in the air of burning skin. It is all true, and it was all horrific. I wondered every day why they didn't send me to the "showers," since I was hurt and not much use to them for physical labor. Perhaps it was like the rest of my entire experience—*just the grace of God*. Though I have no recollection of the name of the POW camp I was in, it felt the same as the other camps I have read and heard about. (It is presumed this was camp Auswertestelle West, as it contained US airmen and was close to the town of Wetzlar.) When Bruce and Dorene brought me and my wife Audrey back to Germany to see the people who had saved my life, I asked them to take me to the Dachau POW camp (also used as a concentration camp), which was similar to the one I was in. I wanted to share with them my experience.

Upon entering the camp, it took only one brief look before everything came rushing back into my mind. My body suddenly became very weak and very hot and moist.

I couldn't look any more. I could barely speak enough to convey to them that they should continue on without me, as I wanted them to see what it was like to have been there. I found a cement slab to sit on, and there I stayed, motionless, consumed in my own memories, as my heart sank for the loss of the many men I had met there, who did not make it out.

Dachau POW Camp

THE WAR IN THE SKY
AIDING THE ENEMY

By Maria Schablass

Staff Sargeant Melvin Stark.

On July 26, 1944, Melvin Stark, an American gunner with a bomber group of B-17s, was flying from Foggia, Italy, to Wiener Neustadt, Austria. In upper Austria, the flight ended. Two German fighter planes shot down his plane and also another bomber. All of the crew on the second plane were killed, and seven on Stark's plane perished. This action occurred near the towns of Ratten and Strallegg.

Allied soldiers who died were buried in the town cemetery. Years later, the Americans exhumed their bodies and buried them in Northern France in an Allied cemetery. Stark and two of his crew had better luck.

His two crew members landed by parachute directly in town. Not hardly wounded or injured, they were captured and taken to the town of Weiz, Austria, where they were turned over to the German Army. Melvin Stark landed in a tree and was nearly strangled by his parachute. He finally freed himself by cutting the parachute cords with his survival knife. Badly wounded, he dragged himself to a house. The people living there decided to take care of him.

County Clerk Maria Schablass remembered July 26, 1944. She had to turn on the sirens for the air raid warning at about eleven o'clock, as the sky was full of enemy bombers.

MARIA

Presently, as I was looking between some houses, I saw two German fighters high in the sky and thought, today, maybe nothing will happen. As I was also a member of the fire brigade, we drove the fire truck deep into the woods to better hide ourselves. Suddenly, all around us clattered and banged. We saw burning airplanes and parachutes as they fell out of the sky. We were very frightened and huddled closer together under the fire engine. Later, after it got quiet, we looked around, and all we could see were the destroyed airplanes. After we got back home, about one o'clock, a friend came by and told me about a very badly wounded pilot near a river.

My first thought was . . . he needs help. I immediately went to the mayor and told him about this. The mayor sent me and the community nurse, another person, and two fourteen-year-old boys to find the wounded soldier. In about an hour of fast walking, we reached the Swieselbauern River and found the injured person lying on the bank. He was covered with blood. First, I had to wash the blood off so the nurse could tend to his wounds. On a map from his survival kit, I showed him where he was. He then showed us a photo of his wife, a good-looking young woman. He then offered us forty dollars to help him. We, naturally, did not accept the money. He then offered chocolate candy bars, which the two boys quickly accepted. I thought to myself, he is our enemy as we are his; maybe there is something in the chocolate? But everything turned out okay. Then, we got Melvin Stark—his name was on his dog tags—on a stretcher to carry him back through the valley. At the lodging of Gasthaus Winkler in Bacher, we could finally put him to bed to take care of him. A doctor who was summoned would explain everything to him with the warning that he would, without fail, be taken to Army Reserve Hospital No. 1. We were then sent home.

A few days later, I wondered what became of him. I inquired and was told, "Don't ask so many questions!" So I didn't ask any more. I just hoped in my mind everything would turn out all right. The next four months, Melvin Stark was a prisoner of war in the hospital in Graz. His leg was operated on by a French doctor. Since no anesthesia was available, other prisoners held him down. An Australian, a Brit, and a New Zealander were some that helped. Because of a shortage of bandaging materials, the doctor used toilet paper as bandages. After his hospital stay, Stark was moved to two different prisoner of war camps. He was freed by Soviet troops in May 1945. Stark thanks all his rescuers as well as all the people of Stralleg, who against odds, risked so much to help him. After his return to the US, Stark sought information from the people of Strallegg about his experiences. He also visited Strallegg in 1978 and was shown everything. The house on Swieselbauern, the path they used while carrying him on the stretcher, and even one of the "chocolate boys," by name of Ernst Schweighofer, whom he met and visited with.

Melvin and Maria.

DIVINE MOMENTS IN TIME

THE EVIDENCE OF GOD

THE FOLLOWING SHORT STORIES ARE JUST A FEW MORE
SHARED EVENTS WHERE YOU WILL SEE
THE EVIDENCE OF GOD.

EVEN THOUGH GOD HAD
WALKED WITH ME THROUGH
THIS JOURNEY, MY HEART WAS
ACHING TO THINK MY FATHER
MIGHT PASS ON WITHOUT
SEEING THE TRUTH IN ME
OR OUR RELATIONSHIP.

RECONCILIATION

By Dorene Stark

Shortly before the events in Libya, my mother had been diagnosed with rectal cancer. As I picked her up to take her to the doctor for her pre-op appointment, my father had fallen on the steps just before I arrived and was now immobile. I was fairly certain he had broken his hip. I brought him to the doctor with us, and he was immediately taken by ambulance to the same hospital where my mother would be admitted the following day for surgery. While my mother was in recovery from the operation to remove her rectum and receive a colostomy bag, my father was a few floors up in ICU. The scans they had taken of him in the emergency room had shown some significant internal issues in addition to the broken hip.

We had no idea his health had been so compromised. He had suffered silently for so many years and now was slowly losing the battle for his life. The complications from an arterial disease were now closing in on him, attacking his colon, and many other organs. He was unable to speak as they had connected him to a respirator. When I went up to check on him and tell him that Mother was in surgery, the doctors informed me of his very grave prognosis.

This came as quite a shock, as I thought we were just dealing with an injured hip.

I begged him to hang on long enough for Mom to see him. I really had a sense from Divine Wisdom, my father knew he wasn't going to make it, and my heart ached for both of them. They were not being given the chance to say their final good-bye after sixty-one years of marriage.

Even though my father couldn't speak, he blinked at me in a way to indicate he understood. We both knew he would do his best to hang on. I felt like his spirit was telling me to go and be with her; he would wait patiently for my return with an update. I stayed with my father until I was notified by the doctor that Mother was in recovery.

As my sister and I sat in recovery with her, we were watching, waiting, and wondering if that moment would come when they would reunite. After several hours, I went upstairs to report her progress to my father. It wasn't until two days later—and countless trips from one floor to another with doctors and nurses calling me with updates and instructions to follow—that their moment of meeting finally came.

We eased Mom into the wheelchair and made our trek up to ICU. You can imagine how difficult it was for my sister and me to try to explain how serious our father's condition was at this time. This might also be their good-bye. As there always is with God, He provided the silver lining we needed, so the timing of this would be perfect as well. My mother was under the influence of post-surgery drugs for pain and anxiety.

Without them, she would have been in an uncontrollable state of a broken heart.

One could noticeably see the relief on my father's face when we entered the room. He knew she was going to make it through just fine. He had done it! He had hung on long enough to say "good-bye." As we wheeled Mother into the cool, sterile room to see her husband rendered speechless with a ventilator, she was in complete shock. She tried to absorb what we were telling her, and then, we left her with him to have their quiet moment together. That evening came, and my father continued to fail. My sister had been staying through the nights with our mother and would do the same on this night after her "good-bye" to him. I called my brothers and suggested they come to the hospital that evening. As I took duty in ICU to sit through the night with my father (my mother was concerned about him being in the room alone), a very strange thing began to happen. Keep in mind he was still hooked up to the respirator, so he could not speak.

As I gazed upon his face, a cold sweat came over me. I recalled in that moment that over the years we had come to have some differences, and hearts were wounded, deeply troubled, and misunderstood. He had cast me aside from the family and condemned me to hell for standing in my truth. Even though God had walked with me through this journey, my heart was aching to think my father might pass on without seeing the truth in me, or our relationship. I knew my father, as well, had an aching heart, filled with his own wounds and sorrow from our past. However, God, in His tenderness, once again, granted the desire of our hearts.

I suddenly felt the presence of the Divine. My cold sweat began to dry. In an instant, my thoughts were filled with my father's voice as he lay there speechless. I felt my heart respond in love. We were actually able to carry on a simple conversation between our spirits. The miraculous piece of this was that God allowed us both to find our resolve and communicate complete understanding and forgiveness. Without a single word audibly spoken, peace prevailed. Our hearts and our relationship were now restored. Isn't it just like our Heavenly Father to provide both of us this sacred reconciliation?

God has already arranged a comeback for every setback,
A vindication for every wrong,
A new beginning, for every disappointment.

JOEL OSTEEN

I stayed watch by his side and witnessed his passing about 3:00 a.m., with no regrets. Welcome to *grace*. It can change everything.

Is there someone you still need to forgive? Have you forgiven yourself? It's never too late, until time runs out. Do you know when that will be?

RECONCILIATION

And He said unto me, my grace is sufficient for thee: for my strength is made perfect in weakness.

2 CORINTHIANS 12:9

Have you ever wondered what grace is? Have you ever wondered what mercy is? Have you ever wondered what the difference is? I have wondered these things for most of my lifetime. Recently, I heard this delineation:

Grace is when God gives us what we don't deserve, and mercy is when God doesn't give us what we do deserve.

UNKNOWN

Breathe in Grace. Let Him kiss your face.

I HAD LEARNED HOW TO FALL
WHEN I WAS A YOUNGSTER,
SO DID MY BEST TO SAVE
MYSELF, BUT THE NEXT
THING I KNEW, I WAS ON
THE GROUND WITH HOOVES
POUNDING WAY TOO CLOSE
TO MY HEAD.

MY HORSE, MY TEACHER

By Dorene Stark

My enthusiasm for horses began at the tender age of six. Through the years, I have been given the opportunity to have these majestic creatures in my life. The lessons they have taught me about relationships, commitments, self-discipline, and authenticity have been priceless. Horses taught me how to use courage with wisdom and strength with grace. They ground me in the midst of my storms. Ultimately, their breath on my face feels like the breath of God.

For the past ten years, I have been blessed with the gift of training a sweet little Arabian, a very dear friend rescued from a neglectful and abusive situation. I am sure you have heard the expression, "Be careful what you pray for." Well, I had been praying for years that someone might have a horse "they couldn't ride." My thought was that this "someone" wouldn't have *time* to ride. What I, of course, had no way of knowing is that out there in the world somewhere, there was a woman who had a horse *quite challenging* to ride. Seemed as if everyone who rode

Dorene riding Stellar Serenity (Siri).

her was bucked off, resulting in a decision not to attempt a re-ride. The owner, Mae, was in a tough situation. A horse that couldn't be trusted was dangerous to keep, not to mention, extremely difficult to sell. There she was, praying for someone who could help her with her horse, and there I was praying for a horse to ride. So, God orchestrated our meeting through a mutual friend. Upon first sight of Siri, my heart melted. In an instant, her spirit filled me with sweet peace. As it turned out, her "sweet peace" would make me another member of her "Flying High" group. After a year or so of riding this very spooky and opinionated little mare, she bucked me off as well.

Out on the trail, there was a broken tree branch. It was sharp like a spear, and it stabbed her right in the side as she swayed into it as we passed by. She began bucking like a crazy horse! The problem was not so much the bucking itself, but when she bucked, my head was in the tree branches. This could have resulted in a blow to my head! I had to make a split-second decision to "bailout" or get clocked by those branches. I decided to bail. I had done this many times in my days of riding, with great success, so why not give it a go again? I took my foot out of the stirrup and threw my leg over the saddle and she bucked again! Bye-bye! Off I went, with heels directly overhead (as witnessed by Mae) and closing in on the ground. I had learned how to fall when I was a youngster, so I did my best to save myself, but the next thing I knew, I was on the ground with hooves pounding way too close to my head. I had felt something splat when I hit the ground. Fortunately, I was able to still move my fingers and toes, which meant there was no paralysis. Good to go! I quickly rolled behind a tree to safety and waited for her to finally calm down. While lying there, I began a quick assessment. I was beginning to feel the pain in my back. The adrenalin had kicked in. No time to waste. Time to resaddle my horse and head for the trailer.

The difference between me and the others before me was I had to get "back in the saddle" again to get back to the trailer. Could I trust her to get me back to the trailer? I had to. There were no other options. There was no way I could walk that far. Calling for an ambulance would take longer than riding back to the trailer and would be far too costly since I wasn't critical. Decision made! Now is where the gift of my animal-communication skills came in handy. I looked into the beautiful dark eyes of this horse, who now appeared to be hanging her head in shame. We exchanged our thoughts through spirit communication. Siri knew I needed her now, and she was willing to offer me the help. My back was beginning to send pain messages, so I got the horse resaddled and gingerly hoisted myself back up. She was amazing. Slowly, gingerly, Siri walked us back to the trailer, even though I was improperly seated in the saddle due to the pain. Normally, this would have set her on tilt.

Here is another praise moment. It just so happened, prior to all this chaos, I had been praying a novena of rosaries to the Blessed Mother. Something our family did from the first to the ninth day of every month. I had just finished my rosary on horseback, literally minutes before our peaceful ride changed. Once again, I had been asking God about this Reiki training I had started. I had completed level 1 and level 2 a few years back; however, I had been feeling tentative about continuing onto the Reiki Master level. In addition, my teacher had moved away, so I would need to find someone local. I needed confirmation that this form of energy work was acceptable and authentic in the eyes of God, or there would be no need for me to continue on. I had gone far enough in the training to have gained the knowledge of what it was and the healing potential it could provide. I was fascinated and intrigued, but without God's blessing and reassurance, I would not go any further in my training. This is how He answered me.

As the pain in my back increased, my initial thought was that I had ruptured my spleen—recalling that when I hit the ground I had felt a "splat." Of course, I was looking toward God, wondering what and why. The message came through: "Use your Reiki." What did I have to lose at this point? If my spleen was bleeding, the Reiki certainly couldn't hurt. After all, now it was His idea. For the next twenty minutes, I held my hand to my back, using the healing energy. A visit to the emergency room gave us the details. The L1 vertebra had been broken. I had expressed my concern about the spleen, but the MRI revealed it was not the spleen. It was actually the bladder.

The doctor then tried to explain what he couldn't understand medically. There were air pockets inside the bladder. He noted this could not happen unless the bladder had been pierced, allowing air to get inside. His confusion came from the fact that he was unable to see any puncture damage to the bladder. He further explained the air would remain contained forever, as it had somehow been sealed off. He was obviously confused, but for me, it was an answered question about God's approval of the Reiki. The energy healing had indeed healed the initial damage.

REFLECTION

As I look back on these events, I am not only grateful, but somewhat amused at the lengths God will go to communicate with me. Do you ever just wonder who's talking to you? I sometimes wonder if it's me, Him, or the devil trying to trick me. He knows I need confirmation that I am listening to Him and Him alone. Sometimes, it comes in a gentle whisper, which has taken ongoing diligence to try to master, and other times, He makes it quite profound.

During my recovery, I was getting a sense there was more to this incident than just the Reiki piece. It seemed there was more for me to learn. As I felt *His* familiar nudge, I was prompted to reach out to a friend, who at times has words of knowledge given from God. During our session, she conveyed several interesting messages to me. One in particular I would like to share. Keep in mind there was very little information given to her, other than me being thrown off the horse. Another interesting to note is I was praying the rosary just moments prior to the "rodeo."

Here was her message:

I am shown a bright cloud of light around you and the horse. There is a very dark cloud above you as well. These energies are creating an incredible force against each other and sucking you in. After the tumultuous explosion, it literally spits you both out together. The message coming through, Dorene, is the beauty in which you both released some negative, emotional history in that moment together.

I had shared with her that my L1 vertebrae was broken and also explained the bladder issue. This lovely lady was my initial Reiki Master mentor, so she completely understood. (She is also Dr. Fisher's wife, who was mentioned in the PTSD segment.) She continued to explain in Native American belief, the back is where we hold our history. This history can even go back for generations. Thus, the reason for their sweat lodges, with their backs to the fire, was to release and sweat out the history. She then suggested that I offer this horse a spiritual animal blessing of Native American tradition. Well, I thought, "How perfect is that?"

After my recovery, I returned to the little mare, with the blessing and a promise that I would not give up on her. I would love her through whatever issues she had. As a rescue, Siri had multiple issues. I felt like we had gone through this together and would continue to work together, so she could enjoy a life out on the trails and learn to love humans again. Prior to her rescue, she appeared to have very little trust or respect for humans. Sadly, after many more months out on the trail, it just didn't seem things were improving as much as I would have liked. I began to question my ability to carry her through this journey any further. Perhaps she needed a professional trainer with more skills and tools than I had in my toolbox.

Things seemed to have plateaued, yet I knew Siri had not fully blossomed in her heart. I certainly did not want to be selfish and deny her what she deserved, yet I didn't want to break my promise and abandon her either. It was time once again to talk to the Creator. I asked for guidance on what to do about this horse. Yes, it may sound like a silly thing to pray about, and I questioned it myself at the time. Remember, however, that Siri was a gift from God. In honoring Him, I also wanted to honor her. I did not want to walk away without His permission. It was another opportunity to let go and let God decide if it was time to give her back to Him. I needed a sign of God's true desire for me, so I asked Him for a sign!

One day, while my husband Bruce and I were out for a ride on the motorcycle, my gaze was up in the clouds as I prayed about this. I asked for clarity. I needed a definite sign to know, without a doubt, whether I should stay with this horse. I asked that by the time we arrived at home, there would be a cloud above our house. It needed to be fashioned in the image of the horse I rode. She is an Arabian breed, with a petite frame and a long, flowing mane and tail. I asked for specifics, so there would be no question or room for my imagination to "cloud" my vision. Ironically, at the time of my request, there wasn't a cloud in the sky. For hours, I looked to the sky off and on, hoping to see a horse, hoping God's desire would be the same as my own. There was nothing. My hopes were deflated, but it was God's will, and I had to come to terms with it. I would now need to explain to Mae I was not comfortable moving forward. However, my heart was sad for Siri. It would be yet another betrayal by a human. God knows best. I had to come to a place of *surrender*. This was all going through my mind as we were heading home.

Upon arriving home sometime later, I completely forgot to take one more look to the heavens! As I walked into the house to put my "leathers" away, the message came through like a bolt of lightning! "You arrived home and never looked up!" Apologizing and feeling completely human and disappointed in myself, I ran outside to the front porch while scolding myself for my negligence and hoping I wasn't too late! I looked to the sky. There it was! Almost too late! I gazed in amazement too long before it occurred to me to take a picture. The cloud was already beginning to get distorted, but you could still see the horse, with the flowing mane and tail.

There was no question about the image. It was a beautiful rendition of a horse in the clouds. I yelled for Bruce to come witness my moment. I needed confirmation that my eyes, through streaming tears, had not deceived me. The expression of complete awe on his face

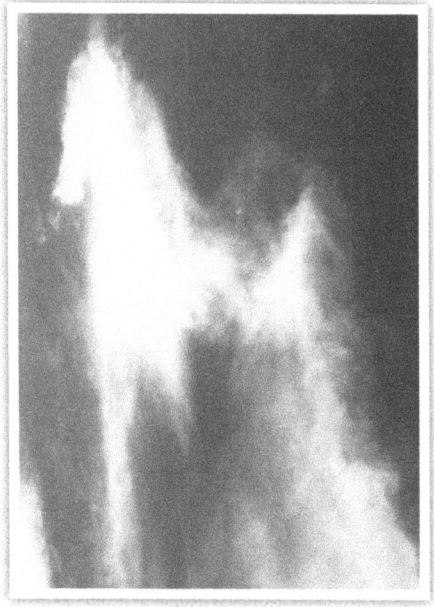

God's beautiful rendition of a horse in the clouds.

needed no further confirmation. Needless to say, I have answered the call, and I am still so blessed to have this sweet horse in my life. She has settled down quite a lot, and it is now such a joy for both of us to get out on the beautiful trails in the Colorado mountains. Though she did not grow into her name until recent years, her registered name would appropriately be Stellar Serenity. It is a unique relationship of blessed friendship and partnership between me, Serenity (a.k.a. Siri), and her owner, Mae. One that blesses all three of us.

Why is this story worth sharing? Within it lies the lessons from the horse, the teacher.

REFLECTION

God is active in every part of our lives. Even in the little things we might think are too small or assume He doesn't have time for. He loves to put a smile in our heart and on our face.

I would have missed the blessing if I had chosen defeat and walked away. First, by using our enemy's favorite friend, fear. When I broke my back, Satan tried to convince me she was too dangerous to ride. After losing that battle, the enemy again tried convincing me I might not be good enough or experienced enough to continue my journey with the little horse I had come to love so deeply. (Fear tried the same tactics regarding this very book, but God had now shown me the lie.) What if I had chosen to believe in these untruths, walking away without asking for the sign of God's truth and desire? What a loss for me and a terrible injustice to Siri. We always have a choice. Such a beautiful example of the love God has for his creatures and the lessons we can learn through them. Honoring them also honors God. It is a show of gratitude for His gifts in nature.

Reflect upon your life for a moment. Doesn't it seem that your most precious gifts came through the most challenging times? The mountain seems to be the steepest the closer you get to the top. Then, you arrive! You receive the amazing gift of accomplishment and embrace the clarity of the view around you. Just think what you would have missed had you turned around twenty yards too early! There's no way to know what is at the top until you arrive. Perhaps it's the race you have entered that becomes more challenging the closer you get to the finish line. Would you turn around twenty yards early and miss the gift of the accomplishment in finishing? No matter how big or small, clarity comes after the journey. The ribbons are awarded after the race. Have you ever noticed the birds still sing after the storm? Perhaps they are reminders that we, too, can sing after our own trials and storms.

We must learn to stand strong against the snares of the devil, who will try to convince us any way he can to give up and turn around. He comes to steal your joy. *God will not lead you where He will not protect you.* Just make sure that He is the one leading you. Keep going!

CAR ACCIDENT

By Dorene Stark

Some answered prayers come in subtle and strange ways, don't they? I found this one to be unique, but certainly not unusual compared to other stories I have read.

I was on my way to the mechanic for some follow up maintenance on my car. I frequently use my car time to carry on conversations with God, and this particular day was no different. Well, at least, that's what I thought when I started out.

I was feeling so much gratitude for this nice ten-year-old Lexus ES I was driving. I was also appreciating the fine bodywork my nephew had recently performed on it to return it to mint-like condition. He had spent numerous hours painting, polishing, and buffing, and his passion for his work shone brilliantly in the sun. It felt and looked brand new! It was my favorite car! It still is quite honestly, though it has found a new owner.

After my session of gratitude, I went on to ask God about my physical pain. I have much history with health issues, including fibromyalgia, and some physical issues from a previous horse accident and a car accident in my high school years. As a result of those accidents, and a lack of proper care afterwards, I have had fifty years of low back and neck pain. Sound familiar? Most of you can probably relate to this on some level. During the past twenty years, I have been led to some wonderful chiropractors and holistic practitioners who have taken me on an amazing healing journey. Even with treatments, however, the medical doctors all agreed the permanent damage over time could not be repaired in the neck without surgery to fuse the disks. My question was, "So God, my back and neck seem to be getting worse with time. I realize this damage was caused from years ago; however, I feel it is *not* your desire for us to live in constant pain, so where do I go with this? I know you have taken the medical field to incredible places. Is surgery the answer? Is this your desire for me at this time?"

I began to change lanes as the traffic around me looked clear. I looked to my right and saw a car that had been hiding in my blind spot. Not anticipating this, I quickly straightened out my car, only to see the car ahead of me was now stopped. I had nowhere to go! I slammed on the brakes, but all of a sudden, they began to come back toward me. I was bearing down with all my might and nothing. It was not the anti-lock braking system fluttering, as the pedal was pushing my leg back toward me. "God!" I yelled out in my mind. "Why are you pushing back the brakes? I can't stop!" CRASH! The sound of crunching metal permeated my ears. My neck came forward and snapped back. "What has just happened?" I looked in the rearview mirror, halfway expecting another jolt from behind, but no one was there. Praise God! This was strange, because it was morning rush hour. Whew!

Next, I saw before me, my beautifully restored car, with a buckled hood, damage to the front bumper, and possibly more. That hurt my heart, but I needed to put things in proper perspective. I quickly did an assessment of my physical state. Seeing no apparent bumps, bruises, or blood, I focused on my neck. This couldn't be a good thing for my already messed up neck. "Strange," I thought, "my neck doesn't even hurt right now. Must be due to the adrenalin. I know how this works."

The gentleman I hit approached my car window as he was calling 911. Fortunately, he had absolutely no injuries either! Praise God! As I was sitting in my car waiting for emergency help to arrive, the most beautiful gift arrived instead. It was Christ showing up as a very welcome guest in my confusion and questions about the brakes, my neck, and lower back. His light filled up my passenger seat; His peace resonated in my spirit. Then, I saw the light take shape as a man sitting in my front seat with a transparent, luminous robe. I began to cry— yes again. (He has a way of doing that, doesn't He?) His arms wrapped around me and all at once turned into the most amazing set of wings, large, beautiful and white, embracing me in His pure protection. My angst about the brakes and why this had happened immediately vanished, and calmness prevailed.

Once again, in what seemed to be an unfortunate circumstance, I found my heart's only desire was to praise the Lord and be patient. I knew this had been completely orchestrated by Him. My first clue was His presence. My second clue was my neck. The pain I had just been talking to Him about before the crash was now gone. I could make a full rotation of my neck, which had not been possible for at least twenty years!

Naturally, the clarity came later as He revealed to me His precious love once again through His incredible attention to the details of our lives in every moment.

I knew I needed to seek out medical attention to assess any post-accident trauma. My first priority was to visit a chiropractor. Upon doing some scans of my neck, the results showed there was no longer a bone spur obstructing a full rotation of my neck. Go figure! God knew exactly what type of impact would be necessary for this release, without harm to anyone else. This explained why my brakes were pushing back at me while I was diligently pushing on them. The gentleman I hit had literally no impact to himself or his car, other than a small dent in his rear fender. My car, on the other hand, was quite buckled in the front. The three different auto body assessors were all puzzled by the fact that my airbags did not deploy with the amount of damage to my car. Each one of them suggested how thankful I should be, as the airbags typically can cause neck, back, or facial injuries even though they are lifesaving. Hmm . . . go figure! Wouldn't it be just like Him to bring in the answer with a bang?

Sometimes His answers are so quiet and sweet. Then, there are those other times, where He knows I need the clarity of something powerful. I am always asking for clarity of confirmation that it is He who is working next to me, and I haven't lost my focus on Him. He delivers in the strangest of ways! Do you see God?

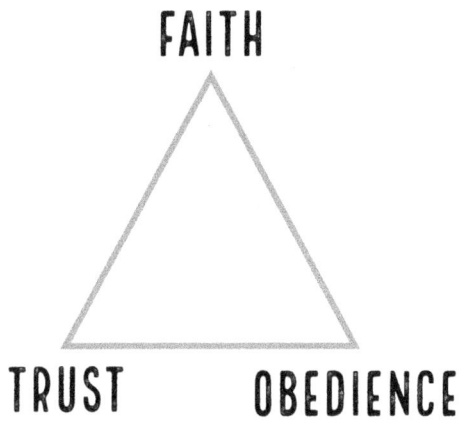

———— ✒ ————

We have given you a glimpse into our lives,
with the hope of bringing you a glimpse into your own—
allowing you to see how God can work thru all of us,
if we will bring Him faith, trust and obedience.

This story might be complete, but God is never done.
He put this book on hold for two years while I (Dorene)
engaged in a life-threatening battle against cancer—
a battle that would bring another series of miracles
and perhaps another book.

———— ✒ ————

A PORTION OF THE PROCEEDS FROM
THIS BOOK WILL BE GIVEN TO THE
TUNNEL TO TOWERS FOUNDATION—
A CHARITABLE ORGANIZATION, THAT SUPPORTS
FAMILIES WHO HAVE LOST A LOVED ONE
IN THE LINE OF DUTY AS A FIRST RESPONDER
OR MILITARY PERSONNEL.